PRAISE FOR *FISHING B*

D0439299

"For anyone who is interested in rel
[Dr. Sawyer] has a way of presenting complex ideas very simply,
which makes this book appropriate for everyone."

Hal Stone, Ph.D., and Sidra Stone, Ph.D.
Originators of Voice Dialogue
Authors, *Embracing Each Other*

"Great common sense, practical advice, and insights without
psychobabble or jargon. Will help many people be far more
successful at love."

Leonard Felder, Ph.D.
Author, *A Fresh Start*
Co-author, *Making Peace With Your Parents*

"This is the clearest and most practical book I've read on helping
people grasp what they want in relationship. It makes us see how
we sabotage our soul's desire. It should be a bestseller."

D. Lindsey Berkson, M.A.
Lecturer; Author, *Women Exposed*

"Colene Sawyer lights the path to healthy relationships. A useful
and clear roadmap to intimacy."

Bill and Judy Elbring
Co-founders – Life Partners, Inc., San Francisco

"*Fishing by Moonlight* offers a way to better understand one's
romantic choices and suggests actions that will improve the
chance of engaging in satisfying love relationships."

Alice J. Sklar, M.A.
Marriage, Family and Child Counselor

Fishing
by
Moonlight

Fishing
by
Moonlight

*The Art of Choosing
Intimate Partners*

Colene Sawyer, Ph.D.

North Star Publications
Georgetown, Massachusetts

North Star Publications
P.O. Box 10
Georgetown, MA 01833
(508) 352-9976 • fax (508) 352-5586

Cover photograph: Peter Menzel
Editor: John Niendorff

Printed in the United States of America

Publisher's Cataloging in Publication
Sawyer, Colene.
        Fishing by moonlight : the art of choosing intimate partners / Colene Sawyer.
        p. cm.
        Includes bibliographical references and index.
        ISBN: 1-880823-12-8.

        1. Mate selection. 2. Interpersonal relations. 3. Marriage— Psychological aspects. 4. Love.   I. Title.

HQ801.S39   306.7'3
                                                                 QBI96-20163

DEDICATION

To my former husbands, John and Phil, with appreciation for the lessons I learned with them.

To my four adult children — Steven, Laurie, Eileen, and Daniel — and their spouses. I have learned enormously from them all.

To my husband, Fred Schlaepfer, with deep love and appreciation. Together we have created the kind of relationship I write about and always knew existed.

ACKNOWLEDGMENTS

I am deeply grateful to the many people who supported, encouraged, and assisted me with this project.

My tutor from Ryokan College, Ben Levine, patiently listened and helped me express my ideas. My good friends in The Inside Edge first helped me test the exercises in this book. Their generous and intelligent feedback was indispensable. The Inside Edge Writer's Group provided support and inspiration. Friends David Lee and Dyane Mohr were invaluable.

My principal inspiration came from pioneering family therapist and writer Virginia Satir and from Dr. Martin Kirschenbaum of California Graduate School, my professor of Family Therapy. The questions that led to my writing this book originated with my fellow divorce counselor and cotherapist, Thomas Burns.

My clients have shared richly of their lives and I have learned profoundly from them.

The final stages of this book have been enhanced by my loyal publisher, George Trim, who saw the book's potential from the beginning. I am enormously grateful to my skilled and patient editor, John Niendorff, who helped me hone my ideas while always honoring them. His perseverance was a match for my own, and his attention to clarity and detail was something to behold!

Finally, I appreciate you, the readers of my book. I have thought about you often throughout this project, as my deep desire has been to share something of value with you from my life experiences.

CONTENTS

PROLOGUE
How This Book
Came to Be Written

Today is my wedding day. My four grown children and my six grandchildren are here to celebrate with me. The groom, my husband-to-be, is exactly who I want and need for a life partner. I am beaming as I walk down the short aisle between the chairs where our families are sitting. Beyond the brick patio, I am aware of the ocean on the horizon and the waves near the beach.

I search for the face of my beloved. Tears of joy and love well up in our eyes as we see each other.

How did this magical moment come about? I know it is not an accident — and certainly not luck. Later I take time to reflect on my life and to remember what led me to this, my happiest day. I recall an occasion seven years earlier, when I was in great pain emotionally. My second marriage, only three years old, was ending. The painful question burning in my mind, keeping me from sleeping on those endless nights, was, "What is going on in me that caused me to choose not just one, but two husbands who were not right for me?"

How could what I feared most — failed relationship and divorce — have happened to me, a marriage counselor, mother of four nice people, daughter of a solid family, granddaughter of a beloved Methodist minister? I knew I could not blame my husbands for the choices I made to marry them. What could I find in myself that would account for what felt like a colossal failure? How might I change it? How might I create the kind of relationship I knew could exist and that I longed for? What had created this life story for me, one so unlike what I expected as a dreamy-eyed bride of twenty-one?

In the anguish of that time, I reflected on my own experiences and on those of others—my clients and friends. I recognized that mine were not isolated questions. Everyone who was in a romantic relationship, or wanted to be, had faced the matter of choosing that all-important person— a mate, lover, or significant other. Could I learn what really goes into making such an important life-decision and distill my understanding of the process to provide increased opportunity for myself and others to make better, wiser choices? Could such an understanding even improve the quality of an existing relationship?

Those questions were the starting point for this book. I was fueled by my own desire to learn how to "get it right" in a romantic relationship, a desire I recognized as important not only for me but for many others as well. My search for answers led me on an extended quest through books, case studies, and experiences with my clients. It paralleled my own inner search for the kind of relationship I always dreamed of, one in which I could be totally myself, one in which I could grow with someone else as we also learned to know each other more and more intimately.

Part of the process of discovery for me has been presenting my ideas and methods over the years in a series of workshops. My students—some single, some married, many divorced or the children of divorced parents —shared stories with me of their lives and romances. The exercises in this book were formed and tested in that environment. (In all of the workshop examples and case histories I cite, I have disguised the identities of the subjects to protect their privacy.) I listened to many hours of reports of joy and pain in relationship. My clients in therapy shared richly of their romantic experiences, their failures and successes. My own life did not stand still, of course, and I also learned from my own romantic experiences. Gradually the ideas I present here developed and the steps involved in producing satisfying relationships became more and more clear to me.

Today, my wedding day, the painful times are behind me. My friends and family reflect my happiness with their own smiles and tearful eyes. This is the most wonderful kind of happiness. My son said to me, "You deserve it, Mom!" I believe he is right, and that is why I want to share what I have learned with you, my readers.

The chapters that follow cover a wide range of human experiences because our choices of partners reflect a wide range of factors. I will share with you some of the encounters and struggles that have taught me and changed me, and what, in fact, is the difference between that dreamy-eyed bride of twenty-one and the happy grandmother bride I am now. I will begin with the experience of falling in love, as seen through the eyes of Emily, my young client.

PART I

WHY WE MAKE
THE CHOICES WE DO

1

YOU FALL IN LOVE, THEN WHAT?

E mily was in love. She had the glow that appears in the first stages of romance. As she bounced into a chair in my office, I saw a vitality and aliveness I had not seen in the five months she had been my client in therapy, since she first came to me following the painful breakup of a relationship.

She brought me up to date with delight.

"My world has shifted. In a lovely, scary, real-unreal, spinning way," she said. "Here's what happened. I went to a convention of a thousand medical technicians. The program had already started. I scanned the meeting room for someone interesting to sit next to. What I was attracted to was the back of a head of dark, wavy hair. I sat down next to him, even though I hadn't seen his face.

"His attention was on the speaker and soon mine was, too. When the presentations were over, he turned to leave . . . and our eyes met. It was one of those magic moments. Either of us could have walked on without a second glance. But we didn't. We jumped into animated conversation about the program. I was attracted to his warmth and enthusiasm. The words tumbled out between us. It seemed as if no one else was in the room."

Emily gave me a look that combined puzzlement and delight. "How do these things happen? I don't know. Was it an accident? Fate?" She wondered aloud if some kind of plan in the universe brings certain people together.

"We decided we had to talk some more," she continued, "so we made a date for dinner the same night. By the end of the meal I realized my world was different. A week later, after our second date, my heart could hardly keep from saying 'I love you,' though my head told me it was too soon.

"Now I catch myself smiling, forgetting where I am momentarily. I notice simple things with new awareness. Colors seem more vivid, music is sweeter. Oh, yes. His name is Ted."

I was delighted by her good fortune, though my knowledge of her prior experiences with relationship caused me to hold some private reservations.

Three weeks later, Emily called for another appointment and came to my office. Clearly, things had changed.

"Last weekend, Ted and I spent the day together. It was intense, wonderful. But toward the evening, I could feel him backing away. He said he was tired.

"The next day he called to break a date and said he wasn't comfortable with what was happening with us. He wanted to ease off. I was devastated. Even more disappointing, I realized that in spite of my originally feeling he was different, he was another 'distancer,' just like other men I had dated. And, in fact, just like my ex-fiancé."

She told me she'd gone from feeling in love to feeling hopeless. Would she always be attracted to men who retreat after a first burst of enthusiasm? Was that situation caused by something she did? By the kinds of men she chose? What could she do so it wouldn't keep happening?

It Can Happen to You

Most of us have run into these difficulties. Perhaps you, too, have met someone exciting and then had a similar disappointment. Or you have thought someone was exciting and then you backed away from the intensity of further involvement. Or you may have experienced other concerns. Perhaps you've already chosen someone, though you frequently wonder *why* you chose this person, because sometimes you don't get along so well. Perhaps you feel trapped by or generally unsure of a relationship. Or maybe you are simply curious about the mysteries surrounding love.

These are some of the issues and dilemmas of romance that I want to explore in this book. The first half is devoted to helping you make discoveries about why you choose the partners you choose. The second half focuses on the next step — what you can do to enhance the choices you make as well as the relationships you create.

The Unconscious and the Conscious

There is a commonly accepted myth that we don't actually *choose* romantic partners — that love "just happens" in some kind of amazing, accidental way. But this is not exactly so, since whether we realize it or not, powerful, unseen forces within us are profoundly influencing everything we do, including the ways we fall in love and our choices of people to fall in love with. These unseen — or unconscious — forces almost always reflect experiences we had early in our lives, along with the feelings that went with them. Even though we don't remember those experiences and feelings, they remain within us, buried in our unconscious. They have their unusual power *because* we are not aware of them. We don't know they exist, so we have no authority over them. In fact, the powerful "chemistry" in romantic attraction often comes from the unconscious. When love "just happens," most of our feelings actually reflect what is going on unconsciously. The process of falling in love is far from accidental.

Nevertheless, the conscious part of us thinks it has knowledge about almost everything, including how and why we fall in love. But these viewpoints about why we do what we do, think what we think, or feel what we feel may not be what's really important as we seek to understand falling in love.

In order for us to have a more accurate sense of our underlying motivations, we must gain access to (that is, become conscious of) as many of our powerful, unconscious messages and memories as we can, so we can use this awareness to make better decisions. Your conscious part may say, "She/he is so attractive and fun to be with I can't resist her/him," but the reasons for your being magnetized to *this* attractive and fun person rather than another one are likely to be hidden in the unconscious.

For this reason, the exercises in this book are designed to give the conscious part of you more access to and awareness of the unconscious part. This will bring you more control over your romantic choices.

First Attraction, Then . . . ?

Between the first moments of strong attraction, or falling in love, and the development of a healthy romantic relationship, some important decisions must be made. This interval is one of the most important and least understood aspects of a successful relationship. As a therapist with nineteen years of professional experience and as a human being who's gone through the ups and downs of several important relationships, I have learned some valuable lessons about this crucial interval, and they may help *you* be more aware and better able to make one of the most important decisions you will ever face—the choice of a life partner. These aware- nesses can also help you create an exciting, growth-producing relationship.

Can You Really Trust Love?

The whole phenomenon of falling in love is shrouded in mystery. What, we ask ourselves, really causes "chemistry" between two people? (Or, as some people call it, being "love sick.") Is it a necessary ingredient in creating a good relationship? How reliable is it?

A broader look at marriage (and divorce) could provide convincing evidence that many of us actually choose a partner who is *not* the person we really want. About half of today's marriages end in divorce. The emotional pain felt by these divorcing couples—and their children—is no doubt producing long-term social problems of which we are only dimly aware. Yet as a society, we still trust "falling in love" as a basis for long- term relationships and marriage.

When we're young and we dream of our future, our hope is to fall in love, marry, perhaps have children, and live a happy life. We don't dream of a broken marriage, the children of divorce, single parenting, perhaps remarriage and the challenges of a stepfamily. When we're young we also may dream of having a family that is happier or more stable or otherwise "better" than the family our parents created. If our childhood family was not as good and loving as we might have liked, we dream of being grown up and having the power to get family life "right" this time — as adults. And we fall in love, trying to do just that. But what is there about falling in love as a basis for marriage that is not working well for many of us?

I'm not ready to give up on love. It can be one of life's most delicious experiences! I believe falling in love is a valid part of choosing a mate and I believe it's here to stay. But *trusting romance without understanding it* is like trusting a small child to lead you through heavy traffic. (Even the words we use, *"falling* in love," suggest risk.) So, as you would use your adult awareness and take that small child by the hand to lead it through dangerous territory, I believe you should take this "smitten self" by the hand when you fall in love.

It is important for us to know more about how we fall in love and choose romantic partners, so we can do a better job of, first, choosing relationships and, second, using our relationships to produce growth and happiness rather than conflict and divorce. While the falling-in-love part is easy and exciting, the reality stage — the time of subsequent challenges in the relationship — is when we can learn more about ourselves and our partner.

Some form of disillusionment, often caused by fear left over from earlier relationships (either adult relationships or those of childhood), inevitably comes up following the initial attraction to a new relationship. That's often when a romance breaks up or fizzles out. So, was Emily and Ted's relationship merely going to be something that "didn't work out"? Were their first feelings of excitement simply unreliable and misleading? Or was something else going on . . . something that, if better understood, could turn potential disappointment into happiness and the fear of pain and failure into greater personal awareness and rewarding experience?

2

UNDERSTANDING
THE HIDDEN LOGIC OF LOVE

I believe we all have a basic need, a mysterious inner drive, that moves us to evolve, to grow as human beings. The things we do may not, at any given moment, seem growth-producing; in fact, we may not even be aware that growth is an option in a particular situation. But there is always a mysterious force moving us toward expansion.

Perhaps an analogy will help. A daffodil bulb, planted in the earth, is driven by its nature to grow toward sunlight. But even if the ground above this bulb were covered with rocks or debris, the bulb would not be stopped. It would sprout and move toward the sun anyway. It would find ways to grow and blossom. As it persisted in doing so, it might have to grow sideways, at an odd angle, or even downward for a short distance in order to continue its overall movement toward the sun. It might not always seem to be growing in the proper direction, but it would be. Likewise, we humans have a drive to grow and blossom into all we can be, though as we deal with the obstacles in life, our progress may not always be apparent.

Part of my purpose is to help people see how difficulties in relationship can serve their overall growth. Indeed, the attraction to someone who challenges you may be unconscious (or seem mysterious and magical). And the growth will not happen automatically, even though you set up the opportunity for it. But the potential is there, and one aspect of the magic and the mystery in your choices of partners, whether it is apparent or not, is that this inner drive to grow is being served. It is one of the elements behind the surprising and often amazing hidden logic of relationship.

WE LOVE IT TODAY, BUT NOT TOMORROW

One of the ways we grow is to choose difficult situations in life, situations that confront us with opportunities to learn and expand. You may ask yourself, "Could I really be choosing problems on purpose? Why would anyone do such a thing?" Yet as we will see, and as I have observed with many couples, the very qualities partners initially find irresistible turn into problems as they come to know each other better. Let's return to the example of Ted and Emily.

Emily, in originally having been attracted to Ted's self-reliance, did not realize that its other, hidden side was *distancing*, the sense of aloofness that later led to her feeling abandoned and fearful. What attracted her at first (self-reliance) is what later created problems (distancing).

Ted, on the other hand, was initially attracted to Emily's openness, not realizing it was deeply connected to her having grown up feeling emotionally alone. When he saw her *neediness*, which seemed to him like clingyness, he was frightened and pushed her away. What attracted him at first (openness) is what later became difficult (an apparent engulfing clingyness).

Here are some understandings that emerged later in my sessions with Emily. She realized that these troublesome qualities in Ted were exactly the same qualities which, when she was growing up, had been parts of her family life and caused her pain. I came to see that the same was true of Ted. Aspects of his childhood that caused him pain were reappearing in his relationship with Emily.

And so it is for most of us. At the beginning of a romance, our partner is an exciting, brand-new person. But I believe part of the excitement of which we are not aware when we fall in love is our recognition of familiar qualities in that person — qualities similar to those of people who were important to us as children. Such familiar qualities remind us of both pain and love from childhood. These childhood hurts came from the same people (our caretakers) we loved and depended on for our survival. Thus pain and love seemed to come from the same source.

For instance, as a child, Ted felt confined and controlled by his lovingly protective mother. Thus, as an adult, he feared relationships with women who threatened to engulf him and deprive him of independence. Emily, as a child, often felt emotionally alone, unnurtured by her busy parents. So, as an adult, she feared abandonment and longed for closeness. She clutched at Ted, which triggered his worst fears: his sense of independence was threatened and he felt overwhelmed. So he distanced himself from her. When Emily recognized his distancing, she was confronted by her own worst fears, as she felt abandoned and alone. Their fears provided a mirror for each other.

The first rush of love obliterated the sources of potential tension between them. They felt only a powerful attraction, a feeling of being kindred souls. They thought this feeling was based on their physical attraction to each other, the interests they shared, and their general sense of excitement in being together. To some extent, of course, it was. But at a deeper level, there was a dim recognition of something else, of elusive qualities that reminded them somehow of childhood. Later, these familiar qualities would lead to troubling questions:

"Is she going to take me over like my mother did?"

"Is he going to be emotionally distant like my parents were?"

Ted and Emily were confronted by complementary personality traits, each of which triggered the other. Their combination of "openness" and "self-reliance" (which later felt like "clinger" and "distancer") represents only one possibility. Other couples may have other combinations, such as "ambitious" and "fun-loving," "emotional" and "rational," "dominant" and "passive," "conformist" and "outrageous," "caretaker" and "receiver." These personality traits may not have been a problem for Ted and Emily before they were a couple, but in relationship the traits showed up as differences.

When Ted and Emily recognized what was going on between them, they began to learn how to use these differences constructively. Ted, stretched by Emily's need for closeness, discovered the part of him that really liked intimacy. Emily's need for closeness helped him to grow in trusting himself in intimate situations. Emily, because of Ted's need for time alone and for independence, grew in her ability to be self-reliant. Her sense of pride in her independence increased. They both found new satisfaction and pleasure in their relationship. And what happened wasn't only that their problems lessened. What happened in addition was that they discovered new levels of maturity in themselves. They had both taken major steps in their development as individuals.

Their having complementary and conflicting personality characteristics was a challenging and ironic situation, yet not at all unusual. This kind of unexpected and apparently coincidental match-up of traits happens more often than most of us imagine. In fact, surprisingly, it not only is present in one form or another in most romantic relationships, but it can also serve an affirmative purpose, which, if understood correctly, contributes to the overall well-being of the partners, individually and together.

Let's look at another example:

George and Kay

George and Kay met at a party. He was attracted first by her flamboyant dress and then by her uniqueness. She did not do what adults are "supposed" to do at parties. She made personal inquiries about his childhood and shared openly about herself. He liked her free spirit. She liked his interest in family and in fixing up his apartment. She thought, "What a refreshing change — a solid, family kind of man."

Within months they were married, but the following year they came to me with problems. Kay had quit her job and was busy with her favorite activities — modern dance and drama. George, who was proud of her talents, liked having her home at first, but then he began to wonder if their goals were too different.

He worked hard at a computer firm and wanted to be able to afford a home. He valued her "free spirit" but wanted her to get serious and work

— like he did, like adults were "supposed" to. The very thing that attracted him to her was causing problems.

In the meantime, Kay wondered if her husband's priorities were "off." Yes, he was a "solid family kind of man," but did he have to be *such* a solid family kind of man? Why couldn't he just enjoy life? The very quality that attracted her to him was now a problem.

The "stretch" to fulfill each other's needs as a way for partners to grow also worked for George and Kay. Remembering childhood relationship patterns clarified for both of them how their affinities later turned into challenges.

George had a beautiful older sister who attracted attention with her charm and talent, and he liked her gregarious nature. But, by comparison, he felt colorless and unimportant. This was compounded by the fact that, as the next oldest child, he often had to take care of the two younger children, and he felt burdened. Having been the "responsible one" in his family as a child, George now felt like the responsible one in his family as an adult.

Kay's childhood was different. An only child of conservative parents, she was adored. She had arrived late in her parents' lives, when they had almost given up their desire to have a child. Her creativity was encouraged in every way her parents could afford, even though they did not have a lot of money. In their eyes, everything she did was wonderful. She could not now relate easily to George's wanting her to do something different from what she wanted to do.

As adults, Kay and George were reexperiencing some of their childhood feelings. George's initial enjoyment of his wife's uniqueness led to his now feeling like a "drudge" (as he was with his sister), while Kay took for granted that her creativity would be appreciated and felt hemmed in by George's wanting her to stop being "her own unique self."

Kay and George grew in understanding, of each other and also of themselves as individuals. They learned to appreciate their differences and why their choice to be together was, to a large degree, because of these differences. Each found some ways to expand, ways that added to the happiness of the other. And, with delight, they discovered that this added to their growth and joy individually.

George began to explore his own creative, fun-loving side. He joined Kay's drama group and painted sets, discovering a whole new part of himself. It was fun for him to stretch, to do something just for enjoyment, rather than for a "responsible" purpose.

Kay developed a plan to use her dancing and dramatic interests by becoming a teacher and being paid for her talents. She gained new self-respect and confidence, as well as new appreciation for George's financial savvy in supporting the family. George could appreciate Kay's important contribution to his life in overcoming the feeling he had carried since childhood of being a "drudge." Kay and George fell in love all over again!

They discovered that part of the excitement — and the challenge — that was so powerfully attractive between them was the feeling they had as adults about their childhood circumstances. They found ways to grow from their differences and this became a rewarding new element in their marriage.

Other Qualities with a Hidden Problem

Emily and Ted represented a "clinger/distancer" relationship. The differences that emerged with Kay and George were "hard-working" and "free spirit" (which later seemed like "rigid" and "irresponsible"). Now that we've seen how this works — how the qualities that initially attract can turn into qualities that cause problems — let's look at some others.

First Impression	Later Discovery
Mysterious	Remote
Dignified	Stiff
Charming	Evasive
Spontaneous	Scattered
Protective	Controlling
Admiring	Jealous

Some couples, in struggling with differences, may find that the problem they have set up for themselves is more difficult than they can, or desire to, work with. Hopefully they will learn this early in the relationship, when they still have a chance to separate relatively easily and find new partners. Others, like Ted and Emily and George and Kay, discover ways to grow together. Helping couples discover whether or not they actually have the basis for an enduring relationship is one of my primary goals in presenting the exercises that follow.

Why do we fall in love with people who present these kinds of challenges to us? Why do we fall in love with people who turn out not to be what we really want? Yes, this can create growth for us and we do want to be all we can be, but the whole matter is still puzzling. And that's why I offer the following information. It will, I hope, help you make logical sense of what often happens.

WE RE-CREATE OUR CHILDHOOD
Understanding Family Systems

Experiences early in our lives have a strong impact on our adult relationships, especially our romantic relationships. This is only natural, since, as children, we learn about love from the people close to us. The next people in our lives with whom we experience anything like that same kind of intimacy and interdependence are our romantic partners. We may be older, but we are not fundamentally different, and familiar feelings and expectations from the past surface again in these new relationships. We are either hurt by them again or we learn better ways of resolving the old dilemmas.

Each of us grew up not only in a family, but also in what today is called a *family system*. A family system is the collection of people in a family and all the events and styles of interaction that are created by these people. It is a collection of all the unspoken rules, behavior patterns, and shared memories from the past. A family system is similar to a delicately balanced mobile, with many parts hanging on threads from slender crosspieces. The mobile's different hanging parts are analogous to family members.

If you pull on one part of a mobile, the equilibrium of the entire structure is altered — though, if left on its own, it will tend to restore itself to the stability that was originally part of its design. Similarly, a family has built-in stability. A particular family system — the mobile — may be one of great beauty, a source of pride, or it may be dysfunctional, in dire need of repair and restructuring. It does, however, have a tendency to stay the same, even though some of its members are strongly dissatisfied with certain aspects of it.

The system creates a very strong bond among its members, one that powerfully affects every person in the family, even if they are separated by thousands of miles. See if you can visualize your family as a system made up of definite roles, mutual expectations, and unspoken agreements. Here are a few examples:

Roles: Boss. Peacemaker. Troublemaker. Hard worker.

Mutual expectations: I cook. You wash dishes. You earn more. I talk more.

Unspoken agreements: If we have money, we spend it. Don't waste food. Sex is not something we discuss around here.

These roles, expectations, and unspoken agreements will become clearer as we proceed and as you have the opportunity to consider your own "family mobile."

Family Systems and Romantic Choices

One aspect of adult self-knowing, then, involves looking at ourselves as part of a family system and recognizing how that system can have a major impact on our ability to make healthy romantic choices. Why does it have such power? Because, in our present relationships, *we tend to create the same situations with which we became familiar in the family system of our upbringing.* So, if we are going to repeat an old situation, we surely need to be aware of what that situation was like for us. (Later in this book you will have the opportunity to create your own "family mobile" and experience other aspects of your family, to help you with this awareness.)

Even if you were determined to create something opposite from your original family, you were greatly influenced by the family system. In one family, for example, the mother insisted that everyone go to church. The oldest, Harry, always silently complied (he is now a deacon). Tom, the middle child, made his mother smile and feel loved, and she accepted his nonattendance at church. Jane, the youngest, was outspokenly rebellious against church. Each of the children, in one way or another, was strongly affected by the mother's attitude.

And now, though they are adults, if Tom (the charmer who didn't attend church) changed and started to comply with his mother's wish, Harry (the conformist) would very likely begin to show signs of being less faithful. At some point, however, the indignation of various members of the family would tend to push both brothers back into their "rightful" roles. This is because there is a direct relationship between each person's role in the family and others' expectations as to how that person will behave. But if the new behavior persisted, the two brothers would have a tendency to complete the role reversal, with Harry finishing his amazing and unexplained drift toward rebellion as Tom embraced religion. The system would come back into balance. (This phenomenon is most obvious in families with a delinquent child who "straightens out," while the "good child" then becomes, or at least is perceived to be, troublesome.)

The fact is, you tend to re-create old scenarios from your family without realizing you are doing so. Even if they are uncomfortable, they feel like "home"—because they are. The loyalties you formed at home led to your developing certain character traits, or psychological patterns, that have more power than most of us generally recognize. You are wise to develop an understanding of these influences so they are not "running the show" without your knowing what is happening.

An old story may help clarify how your family system worked to establish patterns without your awareness. A bridegroom, watching his wife in the kitchen, asked, "Why do you cut the ends off the ham?" She replied, "Because my mother always did." The next time she talked to her mother, she asked, "Why did you always cut the ends off the ham?" Her mother replied, "I don't know. It's what my mother always did." Then the bride's mother called her mother and repeated the question. Grandmother said, "Oh, my oven was too small, so I always had to cut the ends off." Sometimes habits come to us in this fashion.

I have seen family systems reenacted in different ways. Often, for example, an adult will take the role of one parent (either father or mother) and, for a partner, choose someone like the other parent. For example, the two grown children in one family re-created their parents' relationship in the following ways: the older boy became a "peace at any price" person like his mother and married a blamer like his father. The second child, a girl, became a dominator (which is how she experienced her father) and married someone passive (like her mother).

Others re-create the issue they experienced as important in their family system. One woman, who saw her parents fight over standards of housekeeping, married a "neatnik," and though they have an otherwise good marriage, they fight over how clean the house should be.

For each of us, our childhood family is familiar and comfortable. That is one reason for re-creating it. But a more compelling reason, I believe, is the challenge to grow. We re-create that family so we can correct what we feel were the painful mistakes of our childhood, and that permits us to get life right this time, as adults.

DEVELOPING SELF-AWARENESS

As you seek new and expanded awareness about your true motives for entering into a relationship, important clues will come to your attention, clues that disclose the logic behind choices you have made. With this greater understanding about why you fell in love with a particular person, you will be in a better position to make your relationship the very best it can be. That is the purpose of the six-step exploration in the next few chapters. It is an opportunity for you and me to become coauthors in creating an awareness that is custom-made for you.

The first step is becoming clear about your heart's desire, since getting anything is always easier if you know precisely what you want. This is a simple exercise you may have done before, but even if you have, it is important now as a background for the following steps, as we delve deeper into the mysteries of love. Take a few minutes to have some fun with it.

EXERCISE 1: IDEAL PARTNER

Write down a list of all the qualities you want in an ideal partner. Let your imagination go and write as many items as you like. If you have a partner now, set aside your knowledge of that person for the moment and write what, ideally, you would like. After you have written your list, decide which are the seven most important qualities and prioritize them, numbering them from 1 (the most important) to 7 (the least important). Now go back and check every quality that you, yourself, possess. Are there some you do not have? Keep your list for later use, particularly in Exercise 3.

What Are My "Habits of Attraction"?

Let's return to Emily for a moment. She wanted more understanding, which is why she was in my office. She was a perfectly normal person who didn't want to be hurt again, for she had recognized she was headed for a repeat of an old situation. She wondered: could I see any patterns of behavior that were leading her into yet another relationship that seemed destined to fail? Why was she again attracted to someone with the same old problems? Should she avoid making another commitment?

Indeed, sometimes this tendency to re-create problems from the past can make us afraid of commitment to a relationship. At a party, I met a handsome gray-haired man. He told me he had never married. "I'm always attracted to cold, harsh women," he said. "The others aren't exciting. They don't offer a challenge. But I've never had the nerve to marry one of the cold types." Later we discussed his childhood circumstances. With a sense of dawning insight, he described his mother as "cold and harsh."

Could it be that the negative qualities you experienced in important people in your childhood actually do contribute to creating the challenge in a present relationship that is part of the excitement, the "chemistry"? This possibility matches with the previous observation about how the things that attract partners later become problems. How does this operate for you in your present relationships? The next thing you need to know is what your past relationships can teach you. When I first did the following exercise I got some important "Ah-ha!" insights. See what you can learn about your own "habits of attraction."

EXERCISE 2: ROMANTIC RELATIONSHIP HISTORY
On the opposite page, there is a chart for you to fill in.

1.   On the left side of the page, write the names of five to seven people with whom you have had a significant romantic attraction or relationship. You can look as far back as you want in your life. (People often go back as far as grade school.) A "significant" relationship or attraction may refer to its intensity, its duration, or both. List them in the order in which they occurred (the earliest first, the most recent last). If there are more than seven, pick the ones that first come to mind. If there are fewer than seven, just list the ones you can remember.

2.   Alongside each name, in the columns provided, write several descriptive words or phrases about the relationship and/or the person. For clarity, you may want to draw horizontal lines between the descriptions of different people. Use more paper if needed. Try to find words that depict both positive and negative aspects of your interaction with each person. Words related to feelings or specific behavior will be the most helpful. ("Attractive," for example, does not mean much unless it was an outstanding feature of this particular relationship.) Good possibilities might be: open, dependable, affectionate, sexually compatible (or not), matching (or not matching) energy levels, ambitious, competitive with me, the same (or different) interests or goals, arguments, boredom, honesty (or dishonesty), distancing, clinging. "My Predominant Feelings" means the feelings you had most often when you were in the relationship. They may be positive, negative, or some of each.

Consider the above suggestions, but follow your own feelings. Usually the first words that come to your mind will be the most accurate. It's okay to repeat words for the same person or for different people.

Exercise 2 — Romantic Relationship History

NAME	FIRST ATTRACTION	WHAT WORKS (WORKED)	WHAT DOESN'T (DIDN'T) WORK	MY PREDOMINANT FEELINGS	HOW LONG?	WHAT BROKE IT UP?

When you have completed the chart, study what you wrote and do the following:

1. Circle the descriptive words or phrases that appear more than once. Follow the columns down as well as across.

2. Look for patterns or groupings of words or phrases in your answers. What similarities do you find in people you are attracted to? (There may be more than one type or pattern.)

3. Look for what worked and what didn't work to bring you satisfaction. Do you find that you chose the same problem(s) more than once?

4. Who or what usually ended your relationships: you, the other person, or outside circumstances?

5. Reflect on your discoveries from doing both this exercise and the first one (Ideal Partner).

6. Look again at your chart and ask yourself if you recognize patterns among the people to whom you are attracted that are like the patterns of someone else in your family: father, mother, a sibling, a grandparent.

Perhaps you see patterns that resemble more than one person in your past. In my workshops people will often make such discoveries as, "Can you believe it? I married my mother! And she's the one I had the most problems with. Nice people like my dad seemed boring." See what you can find for your own family and relationships. As we go along, how this works will become even more clear to you.

These, then, are the first steps in gaining an awareness of the "unconscious logic" that leads to your being attracted to certain people and not others. (There are other important pieces to add to this puzzle, which will come later.)

If you have not yet chosen a partner, this self-knowledge can be invaluable in assisting you to make wise decisions. Becoming more aware can empower you to use your romantic options to bring about growth and happiness rather than disillusionment and hurt.

If you have already chosen a partner, you can research the logic of what you learned about love in your own past, understand what your partner learned in his or her past, and discover how to give to each other in ways both of you want and need. If you cannot or will not do that for each other, any difficulties between you are likely to continue being problems.

Now you are ready to see whether the partner you actually chose matches the ideal you listed in your Ideal Partner exercise. This is really zeroing in on your choice-making.

EXERCISE 3: COMPARING YOUR IDEAL PARTNER
WITH YOUR REAL PARTNER

On the chart that follows (page 25):

1.   Write the names of your five most significant romantic partners— four from the past and your present (or most recent) partner.

2.   From Exercise 1, copy the prioritized qualities from your Ideal Partner list (most important "1" to least important "7") in order in the numbered spaces on the chart.

3.   Use the "Always/Sometimes/Never" columns on the chart to rate each person on each of your Ideal Partner qualities. Put an "x" wherever appropriate, on a scale from "10" for "always" to "0" for "never."

When you have completed the five names, look at the overall picture. How closely have you matched your actual attractions with your ideal? Is your Ideal Partner list realistic by this measure? Do you need to change the list—or yourself—to attract such a person?

Look again at your chart for Exercise 3. Recognize that you prioritized your list and that the first items are more important to you than later items. Take this into consideration as you reflect on your choices of people. Is there a trend over time toward higher or lower scores for your partners from earlier relationships to now? Did your latest choices match better than your earlier ones?

Sometimes people are upset when they see that their current relationship does not fit their ideal. How can you use those differences, if they

appear, to expand your flexibility and grow with your partner? Can you
communicate your unmet needs to your partner without complaint or
demand? Or do you need to reexamine the appropriateness of your present
relationship?

What can you learn from this picture about the partners you have
chosen to be with and how they compare to someone you would regard as
your ideal partner? If any discrepancies are great, your ideal could be
unrealistic or you might be unconsciously (i.e., without being aware it's
happening) attracted to partners who do not fit your ideal. In either of
these cases, you may need to look more closely at the qualities, familiar
from childhood, that you are trying to find in a present-day relationship—
a relationship in which you want to "get it right" this time.

When I began looking at these factors in my own life, I saw that while
I thought of my partners as quite different from my parents, some
similarities showed up on this chart, especially in my early choices. And
I was encouraged to discover that my later choices were moving away
from some of the problematic aspects of my relationship with family
members and closer to the qualities of my ideal. What do you see as you
contemplate your partners as compared to significant family members?
Sometimes people find they choose partners like one parent and sometimes like the other parent, attempting to resolve different kinds of
problems in their past.

This kind of exploration will help you—as it did Ted, Emily, and the
others whose case histories I discuss — to discover how differences
between you and your partner can become assets that lead to greater
intimacy rather than problems that lead to friction.

Looking into the patterns of your unique experiences with love can be
a most rewarding way to see the pleasures of your past and also to
recognize hurts that may have led to painful choices in romantic partners.
The following chapters will explore these and other issues, helping you
understand how and why you choose your intimate partners and probing
deeper into the mysterious and sometimes amazing "romantic logic" that
brings people together who are perfectly suited to each other — even if
they confront each other with major problems.

EXERCISE 3
Comparing Your Ideal Partner with Your Real Partner

NAME:	ALWAYS					SOMETIMES				NEVER	
	10	9	8	7	6	5	4	3	2	1	0
1											
2											
3											
4											
5											
6											
7											

NAME:	ALWAYS					SOMETIMES				NEVER	
	10	9	8	7	6	5	4	3	2	1	0
1											
2											
3											
4											
5											
6											
7											

NAME:	ALWAYS					SOMETIMES				NEVER	
	10	9	8	7	6	5	4	3	2	1	0
1											
2											
3											
4											
5											
6											
7											

NAME:	ALWAYS					SOMETIMES				NEVER	
	10	9	8	7	6	5	4	3	2	1	0
1											
2											
3											
4											
5											
6											
7											

NAME:	ALWAYS					SOMETIMES				NEVER	
	10	9	8	7	6	5	4	3	2	1	0
1											
2											
3											
4											
5											
6											
7											

3

MORE ON
THE HIDDEN LOGIC OF LOVE

Y ou may understand the drive within you (and others) to grow and blossom into all that you can be. You may recognize how qualities in another person that are attractive at first can become unattractive later on. You may realize that you grew up in a family system whose familiar habits remain with you to this day. But is there even more logic to the mysterious, romantic, magical process of falling in love? The answer is yes. There's a *lot* more, and discovering it will include taking yet a deeper look at what you learned about love in your family of origin.

At this point you may be thinking, "Enough! What I learned about love from the family I grew up in, from living with my parents and brothers and sisters, I don't want to duplicate. I want something better. I don't want anything like that experience." But your *not* repeating that experience is exactly what this new awareness is intended to bring about, and becoming aware of the hidden difficulties in your family relationships is essential if you are determined to learn from them and leave them behind. And what if your own early family relationships were wonderful, loving, and supportive? You will still find this new knowledge helpful, though its principal benefit may mostly be to help you understand others — starting, of course, with your romantic partner.

Unconscious Motives

Despite your determination to do things differently, you may choose a relationship partner who *is* something like your mother or father or someone else from your childhood. That can happen because, as I have pointed out, the logic of falling in love involves the part of you that is unconscious, or outside of your awareness — and that part of you may unwittingly be attracted to someone who repeats a familiar scenario.

The hidden logic behind your selecting certain romantic partners will usually involve three areas: a desire to "get it right this time," a tendency to re-create familiar circumstances, and secret attempts to remain loyal to your birth family. Let's take them one at a time.

GETTING IT RIGHT THIS TIME

A quiet little voice within you may be saying something like, "Now, as a grown-up who can make decisions for myself, I will fix what I didn't like in my childhood. I will have the kind of love and acceptance I always wanted and didn't get from my mother [or father, brother, or sister]. This time, with this new partner, I will get it right." But what we may not be fully conscious of is that part of "getting it right" inevitably involves *choosing someone who has qualities like the person who caused us pain in the past.* In order to "fix" the past, we must have someone who is enough like the original cause of our difficulty to correct the old scenario. Adult love, for example, very often contains an unconscious hope that "now I can have the kind of love I always wanted from Mommy [or Daddy or both]." In order for this hope to exist, the new partner must have some of the qualities we sense as having been part of our own childhood—even if these qualities were troublesome. This provides a challenge that is an important ingredient in creating the excitement we call "chemistry" between two people.

The Good News

The good news, then, is that we choose, often without being aware we are doing so, someone who challenges us to grow, to "get it right this time." This may be the perfect way for us to heal an old pain or feeling of deprivation. If we can get this new person, who is like the old person, to give the kind of love we always wanted and never got, we can feel healed —complete!

Emily, in choosing Ted (who was a "distancer," like her parents were), had the opportunity to learn to be a more self-sufficient adult and to see Ted grow in his ability to include the kind of closeness she longs for. And Ted, in choosing a "clinger" (like his mother was), had the opportunity to learn to accommodate more intimacy and also to have his need for autonomy met as Emily came to understand his needs better. Both will have "gotten it right this time," and each will have learned something valuable in the process. Good news, indeed.

The Bad News

The bad news is that this may be a set-up to fail again. The person you fall in love with, who provides you with an old, familiar scenario, may be someone with whom working this out is impossible. For instance, if the other person is not willing to stretch to fill your needs, or you are not willing to grow to fill her/his needs, the problem will be repeated and you will feel the same old pain. Or perhaps you will choose a situation that makes it impossible. For example, a man in one of my workshops realized he had chosen a string of women who were unavailable—either married or established in a distant area. Finally he realized there was a connection to the fact that his mother had died before he was a year old and he had deeply longed to have her back. Winning one of those unavailable women would be like finally having his mother back, another impossible event. He recognized how he had been setting himself up for failure. Bad news.

The purpose of having a clearer picture of ourselves in the context of our family of origin is to build the kind of self-awareness that allows us to have new authority over our relationships. While family background may have affected us heretofore, it need not control us in the future.

Before we go on, let's look at another example of "romantic logic" — in two generations of a family.

Donna and Larry's Romantic Logic

Donna was a hard-driving advertising executive. At thirty-nine, she had had several romances with successful businessmen. What she really wanted, however, was a man who could encourage her softer side.

When she met Larry, he was a commercial artist selling to her agency. He liked her no-nonsense directness and the humor that bubbled through her. She liked the softness behind his physical masculinity.

Before we explore what happened, let's look behind the scenes to the family mobiles out of which these two people evolved.

Donna's Pusher Mother and Jovial Father

Donna's father was happy and cheerful, and she loved him. Her mother was the "pusher" who got things done. Her father had inherited a family business, and the saying was, "Pop runs the business and Mom runs Pop." It was generally understood that he never lived up to his wife's expectations.

When Donna was little, she could remember feeling as though she had to be "very good." She gave up some of her own free, inner nature to be what she was expected to be, though she was not aware of any of this at the time. She was simply doing her best to succeed in playing her "good girl" role in this family system.

Larry's Nurturing Mother and Demanding Father

Larry's mother was the epitome of loving. His father was a brilliant businessman who always challenged his children to go beyond their limits. For example, Larry remembers his athletic father purposely throwing a baseball just beyond his grasp, forcing Larry to stretch, though he often failed to catch it. While his mother's love was obviously unconditional, he became convinced he would never be quite good enough for his father.

Both of Them Together

When Larry and Donna met, it was as though two halves came together to form a whole. Larry, discouraged about achieving success, took on the easy, nurturing characteristics he learned from his mother. He was also drawn to the reflection of his father he saw in Donna's excitement about work. Donna, feeling pressured always to "be good" and to be successful, saw the possibility of finally being loved the way she had always wanted to be loved by her mother and she also saw the challenge of accepting her more "laid back" father in a way her mother never had. Perhaps they could not have said so at the time, but they both sensed the possibility of "getting it right this time" together.

Familiar Scenarios

Donna: "Will Larry disappoint me like Dad disappointed Mom?"

After six months of dating, Donna began to wonder if Larry's fantasies about becoming a free-lance creative artist rather than doing commercial art were realistic. She began to lie awake at night worrying about his becoming a "starving artist." She remembered the fights her parents used to have and how helpless and afraid she felt as a little girl. Her mother's view of her father as never doing well enough came through despite her best efforts to think it away.

But those were only "middle-of-the-night" fears. She had finally found someone who loved her the way she wanted to be loved.

Larry: "Will Donna push me and never be satisfied, like my dad?"

Larry had his own "middle-of-the-night" fears. He passionately wanted to develop his artistic style without the restrictions that financial success would require. He knew Donna made more money than he did and was proud of the fact, but felt some anxiety about it. When they discussed the matter, she said she wanted him to do what he wanted to do. But Larry could feel the way Donna pushed herself, and he did not want to be pushed like that. He wanted his accomplishments to be "good enough."

The joining of Donna's and Larry's family systems contained several challenges. They had each felt something not quite balanced in the "mobile" of the families in which they grew up. Both wanted to improve on their perception of what was not quite right and, as adults, get it right this time. Each unconsciously recognized the excitement in the opportunity to take old elements and make something new and beautiful. And they recognized, if only dimly, that the very things that attracted them to each other also had the potential to become problems and to separate them.

Donna's challenge was to accept Larry's love and trust him to do what was right for him—not to push him in the way she had pushed herself and in the way her mother had pushed her father. Larry's challenge was to continue to be loving like his mother and at the same time stay true to his own goals and gain confidence in his own accomplishments, rather than giving up as he had often done with his achieving father.

These were difficult issues, requiring considerable change from the patterns Larry and Donna grew up with. Just as they could provide exactly the learning each partner needed the most, they could also hold the seeds of the same old unhappiness.

RE-CREATING FAMILIAR CIRCUMSTANCES

There is a tendency for the family mobile—the family system—to return to its original design or to re-create familiar circumstances when we establish a new family. There is a "magnetic pull" to the old situation, even if it is not an ideal one. This tendency to repeat old scenarios has a powerful effect on our relationships.

What happens to people who win a lottery and are thrust suddenly into a new financial status? First they rejoice, but years later most discover they have found a way back to their pre-lottery lifestyle — one that is comfortable and familiar. They have found ways either to spend, lose, or give away most of the money or they have simply maintained familiar circumstances in spite of the extra money. This is exactly what can happen to intimate relationships, as partners tend to re-create old, familiar, personal situations, even when those situations seem less than ideal.

We have already discussed the tendency to choose mates who have the familiar qualities of a particular parent. Beyond that, there is also a tendency to re-create the familiar environment or "mood" of our original family. These moods could include depression, a feeling of lack (perhaps of money or social acceptance), a quiet or noisy atmosphere, a dread of illness, or a sense of artificial optimism. If this situation, now re-created in the present, does not match the idealized version of what we want, we may blame our partner or our circumstances, not realizing the role we have played in unwittingly choosing this familiar atmosphere. The cliché "It's not much, but it's home" expresses this tendency to gravitate to the familiar.

There are several ways to re-create the familiar mood of your family situation. For example:

Sara and Leon

Sara and Leon fell in love almost at first sight and married very soon thereafter. But after their initial year together, they were both unhappy with their relationship, and each felt it was the other's fault. Though they "looked good" in public, in the privacy of their home they created a gloomy atmosphere. What they discovered in therapy was that though their families were different on the surface, both were rigid, depressed, and more prone to criticism than praise.

That was the comfortable, familiar ingredient they recognized in each other. Both had hoped to create a very different kind of family, but each brought old "mood expectations" to the marriage. With their recognition of this as the problem, they could work constructively together and begin to create a happier environment in their home. This required conscious, determined behavior changes from them. Blaming gave way to expressions of appreciation. Demands gave way to requests for what was wanted and needed. The original excitement began to return. Leon said later, "To think I considered giving up on our relationship because I wasn't getting what I wanted. I was half the problem myself, and being away from Sara would not have solved it. We have more to learn from each other, and that's exhilarating!"

SECRET LOYALTY TO YOUR BIRTH FAMILY

Another element that is important in understanding your reasons for choosing certain partners and for relating to partners in particular ways is family loyalty. Family loyalties, for instance, may cause you actually to choose a beloved intimate partner to be a scapegoat.

Do you know the old song "It Had to Be You"? It expresses the feeling we often have about someone we love. We love the person but are, at the same time, annoyed, exasperated, perhaps even angry because of the things he or she does. We don't like ourselves much, either, when we are grouchy or mean to the one we love. Yet we know that, difficult as the person may be, this is the right person for us. The phenomenon is confusing and perhaps can only be understood in the context of family history.

The gift of life itself, which includes the care we received as young, dependent children, leads us to feel a sense of obligation and loyalty to our parents. These feelings, whether we are aware of them or not, are a powerful part of us. If we were fortunate enough to have received appropriate and tender care — if our parents gave us nurturing, support, and inspiration as children — we are likely to feel a desire to return the love we received. This desire may be felt not only in regard to our parents, but may also extend to our partners, our children, or society at large. It can give meaning and richness to life.

However, a lack of nurturing and inspiration in our family can have created just the opposite effect. Many of us believe our parents failed in some way to give us what we needed and that we were deprived. While we may feel obligated to be caring and loyal to our parents because they gave us life, we may also experience considerable resentment toward them. Because of that basic obligation, however, we are often reluctant to express our negative feelings *directly to our parents*. (This ambivalence can be seen in its full form if someone who is not in the family criticizes our parents. Even if we believe our parents deserve the criticism, we tend to rush to their defense.)

What happens to those resentments we feel? In our need to protect our inner image of our parents, we spontaneously take those resentments out on others, especially intimate others, with whom we feel safest when doing so. We take out on a romantic partner the resentment we really feel toward our mother or father, thus being able to vent our feelings while still remaining loyal to our parents.

For example, one female client said, "I've been noticing that I have loving feelings toward my dad, yet another part of me remembers he was an alcoholic and often mean to me. He's a lot of the reason I'm in therapy. It feels weird to have these loving feelings toward him at the same time I also have negative memories about him. And I'm beginning to realize that I take out my angry feelings about him on my husband. I even create the same issues I had with my dad and get furious with my husband over them. I want my marriage to work, but these old feelings are getting in the way."

Her situation illustrates how — often without our being aware of it — we displace our difficult feelings toward parents onto intimate partners. This usually appears after the first blush of romance, even though the unrealized recognition of qualities similar to those of a family member was part of the initial magical chemistry.

Old, unresolved resentments toward parental figures (or toward former partners who caused us pain) often come out unexpectedly. They emerge in blame. "It's his fault . . . " "It's her fault . . . " "If she would just . . . " "If only he didn't . . . " "Why can't she at least . . . ?" "If only you would . . . then I would . . . . " Blaming your parents or former intimates may even be justified, but expressing it to intimate partners in the present is not going to produce the love you want, especially if the real problem is a situation in your past.

While the scapegoats we are considering here are romantic partners, we should realize that they may also be children, bosses, employees, or even groups, such as people of different races, religions, or nationalities. Finding scapegoats is easy. What's often difficult, however, is admitting, or even being aware, that the primary sources of the resentment are the people who were very important to us when we were young.

How Past Hurts Create Current Resentments

Resentments from childhood can produce difficulties in romantic relationships and even in relationships with friends or coworkers. For example:

Deborah came to me for therapy because of an unsatisfactory love affair. She talked about being unable to control her anger, especially when she was disappointed by her lover. Her rage could erupt whether he was present or not — in public as well as in private. Because she had worked very hard to achieve her position as a business executive, she didn't want to jeopardize her career with inappropriate emotional displays in front of others in a professional setting. She was frightened to realize that her responses were often out of control.

Her love affair ended. As the emotion from the romance subsided, Deborah realized that her problems had not been resolved with the end of that relationship. She began to talk about her boss, reporting arguments with him that were similar to differences she had in the past with her ex-lover. One day she had a dramatic argument with her boss, screaming accusations at him. She recognized later that her rageful feelings were similar to those she felt with her former lover and with other men in her life. She felt justified in having behaved as she did, but that behavior had significant consequences: she was asked to leave the company.

Deborah found another position. But soon she was reporting to me the inadequacies of her new boss. The situation became very difficult and was made worse by an altercation with a male coworker she regarded as incompetent.

She was, however, beginning to realize the problem was hers, not just the coincidental appearance of men with whom she inevitably argued. She further recognized that these circumstances were virtual duplicates of past situations with her mother and father. She wanted to deny that her childhood had anything to do with the present, but as she delved into her past feelings, the connections became unmistakable.

Deborah was always on guard to be sure she was being treated fairly. Where did this come from? As a child she felt frequent disappointment at the unpredictability of her alcoholic mother. Also, she had been told many times that when she was born her father cried after he was told she was a girl. He openly favored her younger brother, adding to her feeling that girls would not be treated fairly. Deborah used the rage she felt in her youth to motivate herself to build a career in a "man's world."

Only now did she see how her childhood feelings caused her always to be on guard so she would be treated fairly. She began to be aware of the old feelings of disappointment underlying her anger. Gradually she learned how her own behavior, "right" though it might have felt, created her difficulties. In her personal life, she began to be more realistic about romantic relationships. Instead of launching into the rage that previously overwhelmed her, she became increasingly conscious that her sadness about her father's rejection and her mother's unavailability was the real, underlying cause of her intense emotions.

The old feelings of rage, then sadness, still appear when she feels unfairly treated or abandoned, but she is working to be more aware of her emotions, how they have affected her relationships, and how she will need to put them in better perspective in the future.

Loyalties that tie you to your past may be an asset or a liability (probably some of both) in choosing and relating to a romantic partner. The important task for you is to separate the blame or resentment that belongs in your past from current problems, so it does not interfere with your present happiness.

In your attempts to find an appropriate scapegoat or a person who is similar to someone who hurt you in the past, you may have found a person who clearly does not match your own criteria for an ideal partner. The partners you have actually chosen may reflect your past more than your present wants and needs. Thus you may, in the words of the old song, "always hurt the one you love," yet feel as though "it had to be you." If you look back to your work with Exercise 3 (Comparing Your Ideal Partner with Your Real Partner) you may see differences that come from your unconscious choice of someone to be a scapegoat for your resentments from the past. This may be logical in terms of your unconscious needs but not logical in terms of creating a successful relationship.

For most of us, re-creating a less-than-ideal familiar family scenario without being aware we are doing so can be a dangerous trap in romance. Becoming conscious of our own family-inherited situations and moods can help us learn the available lessons rather than continuing to create the same old painful scenarios. Awareness is the first step in changing our behavior so we can create the kind of love we long for.

Having grown up in a healthy family may lead to one's easily forming satisfying relationships. What is already familiar, rather than being difficult, is seen as desirable and workable. People with this fortunate heritage might say, "What's the problem? You just fall in love and start being with the other person. Of course you have to behave in a way that enhances the relationship, but that comes naturally."

However, it "comes naturally" only if it is a familiar experience from our own family background. Otherwise it must involve new learning, consciously undertaken.

"Rescue Marriages"

In her book *Good Marriages*, a study of successful couples, Judith Wallerstein describes what she calls "rescue marriages." In this type of relationship, two people with difficult childhoods and no positive role models for marriage choose each other to share the vision of creating the kind of family both long for. Because they share the need for healing old hurts and they agree to help each other with the problems that come up from their pasts, they are able to create a healthy marriage. They are determined to create the kind of emotionally positive environment for their children that they, themselves, did not have. The pain of their own pasts drives their determination not to repeat it. These marriages may be stormy, but the partners have a strong, loving bond and support each other and their children. The choice of a partner who shares this vision and is willing to do what is necessary to make it happen is an important ingredient in creating one of these good marriages.

Can Childhood Resentments Be Released More Safely?

If you have been hurt, giving up your negative feelings may seem difficult and sometimes impossible. But by first discovering these feelings and then finding ways to release them safely, you can avoid aiming this negativity toward the wrong people — either your intimate partner or others who are inappropriate targets. How do you go about releasing these feelings? In general, you find a way to reexperience them—to say, write, or act out the sadness or fear (often first experienced as anger) you could not or did not express when you were young and powerless. Sometimes expressing these feelings directly to the parent or other person you hold responsible for your hurt feelings may be appropriate, but more often, expressing them with someone else, someone you trust, is just as effective and less apt to cause further harm. If the reservoir of unexpressed feelings continues to damage your relationships in ways that seem beyond your control, you might want to consider hiring a therapist to help you heal this past pain. You will find more information about this in chapter 10.

Your next step in working with issues from the past is to create your own family mobile. This will give you a complete, personal picture of how your family influenced you and thus your romantic choices.

EXERCISE 4: CREATE YOUR OWN FAMILY MOBILE

The easiest way to do this is simply to follow the example on page 41. Take a piece of paper at least 8½" x 11" in size. At the top write "My Childhood Family." Now look carefully at the example. Make your drawings two or three times larger than the model, so you will have plenty of room to write.

Be sure to give yourself sufficient room to include everything necessary (such as, for instance, if there have been many marriages or many children). Squares indicate males; circles, females. Show relationships in these ways:

1. Marriages and divorces: The solid horizontal line between partners indicates a marriage that exists or that existed until death. A broken line indicates a divorce. (Unmarried partners who live together may regard their relationship as permanent and elect to indicate it with a solid line. Unmarried partners who had a child but are not presently in a relationship with each other should indicate their circumstance with a broken line.)

2. Children: With a vertical line, connect them to the line that connects their parents. List them, in order, from oldest to youngest.

Include only the biological family in each case. (For example, do not include the spouses of brothers and sisters, but do indicate the family as it existed when you were a child.) Do include yourself. Multiple births may be indicated with circles and/or squares on a horizontal line positioned to show sibling order. Include all births, even stillbirths.

3. Deaths: People who are now dead are indicated by a diagonal line drawn through their circle or square.

4. Descriptions: After the mobile is drawn, write the name of each person in the appropriate circle or square. Next, write three to ten words or phrases near each person's circle or square, describing that person. You can do this quickly and simply, reflecting the first things that come to mind. If you didn't know some of the people in your family very well, or at all, use whatever information you have been told or have guessed. You may be surprised at how much you can infer. Or you may be distressed at what you do not know. At least you are now more aware of the missing pieces and perhaps you can ask questions to get new information about them. Having complete information is not necessary, but if it is available you may benefit from it.

5. Family Rules or Values: After describing the members of your family, make a list on each page of the "rules" or values that were important to them. Such rules would ordinarily deal with common family things/functions, such as food, money, sleep, work, education, grades, play, sexuality, housekeeping, secrets, who is the "boss" of what, and so forth.

Some of these are rules that would be spoken. Some would be understood and unspoken. You may have to think about it a while even to be aware of them, but they can be very important. For example, if there is some kind of addiction in the family, such as alcoholism, an "understanding" may exist that this is a family secret. Abuse of any kind may be tolerated, but also be a family secret. (Of course, these charts are for your use alone, so don't hesitate to make them as complete as you can, thereby allowing you to gather as much information for yourself as possible.) Some other examples of family rules that may be spoken or unspoken:

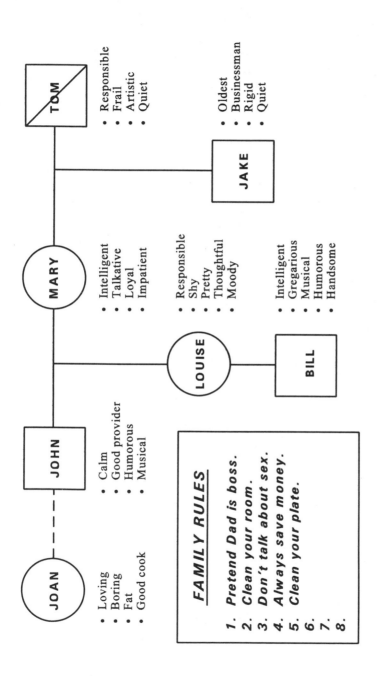

JOAN
- Loving
- Boring
- Fat
- Good cook

JOHN
- Calm
- Good provider
- Humorous
- Musical

MARY
- Intelligent
- Talkative
- Loyal
- Impatient

TOM
- Responsible
- Frail
- Artistic
- Quiet

LOUISE
- Responsible
- Shy
- Pretty
- Thoughtful
- Moody

BILL
- Intelligent
- Gregarious
- Musical
- Humorous
- Handsome

JAKE
- Oldest
- Businessman
- Rigid
- Quiet

FAMILY RULES

1. *Pretend Dad is boss.*
2. *Clean your room.*
3. *Don't talk about sex.*
4. *Always save money.*
5. *Clean your plate.*
6.
7.
8.

Exercise 4 — Creating a Family Mobile (sample)

- *"We don't like rich people."*
- *"Don't let the neighbors [or outsiders] know."*
- *"Children should be seen and not heard."*
- *"If you misbehave, you'll get spanked by Dad [or Mom]."*
- *"If you don't get an education you won't amount to anything."*
- *"A woman's place is in the home."*
- *"Hard work pays off."*

If you grew up in the 1960s and were influenced by the sexual revolution or the feminist movement, you may have rules that are quite different from some of these examples. Comparing yours to the rules your parents grew up with will be interesting.

If you grew up in two families, with two separate households, you might have two sets of rules and need to make two lists (interesting to sort these out!). They would include the same kinds of "shoulds" and "shouldn'ts"—either spoken or unspoken—that were described above for family rules.

Grandparents' Generation

We will go into more detail later about how to use the Family Mobile, but first, now that you see how to do them, go back one more generation, to the one that also had great influence on who you have become—your parents' parents and their families. This may be easy or may stretch your memory. If you can't remember certain things, even recognizing that the information is missing may be important for you.

Take another piece of paper (don't use the back of your first mobile, because you will want to see them together). Write "Mother's Family" at the top. Then go back, follow the steps above, and create a mobile for your mother's family. Do not include the spouses of your aunts and uncles— only the family that existed as your mother was growing up. It will probably be challenging to discover the rules for her family, but most people can at least come up with general ones. The rules of your parents' generation may be different from yours, or you may see some similarities. Nevertheless, the important thing is to be aware of the rules with which your parents were raised so you can see the patterns that affected them, since they were the most influential people in your life.

Now . . . you guessed it. The next step is making a mobile for your father's family. Repeat the same steps. It should be easier this time.

Many people (myself included) discover they don't even know the first names of some grandparents or of parents' siblings. This may even be distressing. Perhaps you can use it as an incentive to ask some questions of relatives or old family friends. Or you can simply put down what you know and make intelligent guesses about the rest. You probably have some idea about whether these people were rich or poor, from the city or country, educated or not, and what part of the world they lived in—all of which will give you clues about their values and family rules.

Only one step remains. If you are married or have ever been married or had a child, you will want a mobile of your own adult family. Depending on your age and experiences, this may be simple or complex. Certainly, though, coming up with the information will be easier.

When you have completed drawing your Family Mobiles, spread them out on a table or on the floor. Look at the similarities and differences in the families that directly affect you. Do you see patterns going through the generations?

Answer the following questions for your own information. Please do this carefully, being aware that even one or two "surprising" answers or previously hidden facts may reveal whole new, perhaps life-changing, areas of information with regard to your relationships. You may want to write down your answers, go over them aloud with someone else, or simply think about them yourself.

1.   In each generation, who conformed to the family rules and who rebelled? Was there a difference for males and females? Did this change or stay the same from one generation to another? Answer this for both your mother's family and your father's family and see if your childhood family was more like one or the other. For example, among any rebels or conformists, are some like father? Like mother? Are there addictions (to food, alcohol, drugs, sex, work, etc.) that repeat themselves through the generations?

2. *In regard to the siblings in each family: did they, in general, grow up to be similar to or different from parents? More like mother or father? Are there differences among males or females?*

3. *What qualities in your parents' families and in your childhood family do you value most? What qualities have been most troublesome for you to deal with?*

4. *With which parent did you have the most difficulty? What specific qualities were problematic for you? Have your romantic partners had any of these qualities? Have you chosen partners specifically because they were different from your parents? Have you later discovered similarities that you were not aware of when you met?*

5. *With which parent did you align yourself? Did you choose partners more like that parent or more like the other parent — or like a sibling, grandparent, or other important person?*

The next chapter will provide you with an opportunity to get more in touch with childhood patterns that affect your adult relationships. You will collect more personal data, which will help you recognize your habits of attraction.

4

REEXPERIENCING FAMILY PATTERNS

We have examined several dimensions of "romantic logic." Now we are ready for two exercises that will round out your understanding of how you choose romantic partners. This will complete the initial six exercises and prepare you to summarize your results.

WHAT ABOUT CHILDHOOD?

"Tell me about your childhood."

This request may inspire a flood of memories, a blurred recollection, or a complete blank. Regardless of how you respond, childhood is one of the most important periods of your life to explore, because the lessons you learned about loving then have a powerful effect the choices of romantic partners you make now, as an adult. Therefore, it is important for you to revisit the childhood scenarios that provided the background for what you now want and expect from intimate loving.

The following exercise, one that builds on the previous exercises, encourages you to reexperience memories of childhood and of the relationships in your family. This, again, is an opportunity for you to personalize the information I have presented and make it individually meaningful to you. Doing so will help you to pinpoint your own individual emotional needs in a relationship. The questions include considerable detail, which serves to intensify the process.

This exercise has a different format than the previous ones, as it presents a series of prompts to your memory. You may read through the questions alone. However, to have a more powerful and useful experience, I suggest you ask a friend or family member to read them to you, so you can close your eyes and focus on the memories. Another way to accomplish the same thing is to read the questions into a tape recorder. Then when you play the tape back, you can use the pause button to regulate the speed of the session.

Though the exercise can be completed in twenty minutes or less, you might want to allow more time so you can talk it over with your "reader," write about it, or contemplate it. At the end of the exercise, you will find two questions that require short, written answers. Your reader can read them to you. Have paper and pen nearby, ready to respond.

In preparation, find a quiet, private place where you won't be interrupted. Whether you read the material yourself or have another person read it, be sure there is sufficient time between each question for the memories that come up. Do not talk during the exercise; just experience what's going on within you. If you are using a reader, work out some simple hand signals that will tell the person to go faster or slower or to pause as you require, so you don't have to interrupt your concentration by saying anything. Of course, if you are using a tape recorder, you can press the pause button to regulate the speed of the session.

As you go through the exercises, you may notice conflicting feelings. This is not unusual. Try not to push away any discomfort. Allow yourself to have the full range of your reactions.

Now . . . make yourself comfortable. Close your eyes. Begin.

EXERCISE 5: REMEMBERING CHILDHOOD

Picture yourself as a young child. Pick a specific age, preferably between four and seven, a time you can easily remember. Try to stay with one age, but if experiences from other ages come to mind, simply notice them and go on.

*Imagine how you appear as a child: hair, clothes, build, height . . . .
Imagine standing in the front of your home (if you lived in several places
during those years or if your memories are indistinct, pick the earliest
home you can remember fairly well). Let the feeling about that place come
over you . . . . Listen for sounds . . . . Now imagine going into this familiar
place . . . . See if you can recall how the rooms are arranged . . . . In your
imagination, go into the room where you sleep. Notice colors . . .
arrangement of the furniture . . . windows . . . . Touch something, perhaps
sit on the bed . . . .*

*Remember getting into bed at night. Did you have a favorite toy or
blanket . . . ? A thumb in your mouth . . . ? How does it feel . . . ? Do you
hear anything . . . ? Do you share the room with someone else . . . ? Do
you argue with anyone in this room about space, toys, neatness . . . ? Are
secrets here . . . ? Do you cry here . . . ? Does anyone "send" you here
. . . ? What sense of yourself do you have in this room?*

*Now go into the kitchen . . . . What do you see . . . ? What do you hear
. . . ? What do you smell . . . ? What do you taste . . . ? Who is here with
you . . . ? Are you helping with something . . . ? How do you feel in the
kitchen?*

*Now go into the living room. Who is here . . . ? Recall the furniture
arrangement . . . . Is the radio or TV turned on . . . ? Sit in your favorite
place or a place you remember . . . . How does it feel . . . ? If there is a
family room or playroom, go there . . . . Recall the activities there . . . .
What do you feel in this room?*

*Now remember the people who live in the house . . . . Focus on your
mother [or female caregiver] . . . . How does she look . . . ? How does it
feel to be near her . . . ? How does her touch feel . . . ? What do you
remember her saying . . . ? When does she leave the house. . . ? When does
she return . . . ? Recall her face and her words when she was loving . . .
when she was angry . . . . Do you associate her with any particular aroma
. . . ? Let yourself remember your feelings about her . . . .*

*Now concentrate on your father [or male caregiver] . . . . How does
he look . . . ? When does he leave the house . . . ? When does he return
. . . ? How does his voice usually sound when he talks to you . . . ? How*

*does he sound when he is the most loving . . . ? How does he sound when
he is angry . . . ? How does he show that he cares about you . . . ? Does he
read to you . . . ? Does he play games with you . . . ? Do you associate him
with any particular smell . . . ?*

*Now imagine Mother and Father [or caregivers] together . . . . Look
at their faces . . . . Think of a time when they are . . . angry . . . worried . . .
loving . . . . Do they touch each other . . . ? How do they touch . . . ? What
do you feel when you see them together . . . ?*

*How do their voices sound when they talk with each other . . . ? What
are they saying . . . ? How do they talk about you . . . ? How do they talk
about money . . . ? Do they ever talk about sex . . . ? What other things do
they talk about . . . ? What do they argue about . . . ? What are you feeling
as you remember Mother and Father together . . . ?*

*Remember a typical evening meal in your family . . . . Who is there
. . . ? What is the conversation . . . ? The aroma . . . ? The flavors . . . ?
How do you feel . . . ?*

*Take a few moments and allow any other memories of this time and
place to emerge . . . . Any sights . . . ? Sounds . . . ? Feelings . . . ?*

*Take plenty of time to complete this childhood experience. When you
have finished, feel your adult body now, here in this room. Begin to move
a little. Take a few deep breaths. Imagine how the place you are in now
looks. When you're ready, begin to open your eyes and move even more.
Finally, return your attention entirely to here and now.*

*After you have finished the exercise (and without talking), write down
the answers to the following questions. Write words or phrases or a
sentence. Whatever first comes to mind will be the most useful. Writing
long or elaborate responses is not necessary.*

1. When I was little, I most wanted someone in my family to

_____

2. When I was a child, the thing that upset me most was

_____

Label your answers "Exercise 5" and keep them with your other exercise results for later use. Always be certain to return your awareness fully into your body and to the present moment when you finish any of these "memory" exercises. Be alert for any "spacy" feelings, and if you feel lightheaded or in a dreamlike state, simply breathe some more and move around. Often having a snack will bring you back to the here-and-now.

There is one more exercise in the initial six-part series. After completing it, you can put all six parts together to see a whole picture of how you choose romantic partners.

GRANDPARENTS

We have considered grandparents as a part of your family mobile. That may be seen as the "data-collecting" part. Now you will have an opportunity for an experience of them, in memory, as your parents experienced them. Even if you did not know your grandparents, they may have had a powerful influence on you. For example, one of the events that shaped my life was the sudden death of my father's father, which happened when Dad was twelve years old. When his father died, my dad had to go to work to support the rest of the family. This meant he did not have the kind of adolescence most of us have. No wonder he couldn't understand what it was like for me when I was an adolescent! Many years later, when I was able to put myself in his shoes and understand what life was like for him when he was an adolescent—having to work instead of being with other young people in social situations—I began to understand what his father's death meant to him . . . and to me.

In my workshops, this is often seen as the most worthwhile exercise we do in stretching beyond our usual experiences and getting in touch with parts of the past in new ways. It is also seen by some as challenging.

See what it is for you. You may need to use your imagination to fill in missing information, but don't be concerned if you are not able to recall some things. You are mainly interested in emotional highlights, not exact details.

As before, if you don't have a reader help you, this can be read alone or into a tape recorder. But if you do have someone read it to you, you can concentrate on the questions and have a more meaningful experience.

This exercise has four parts. First, you pretend to be your mother (or female caregiver) and you answer questions about her mother and father. Then you pretend to be your father (or male caregiver) and answer questions about his mother and father. As you do this, you may be surprised by how much you really know about your father and mother and their relationships with their parents.

If you were adopted as an infant or toddler, please use the parents of your adoptive parents, since your adoptive parents are the ones who most affected your life while you were growing up. If you were raised by only one parent, you may try to do this exercise for the parent you didn't know, as well as for the one who raised you. If the information you have is extremely sketchy, you may decide that doing the exercise for both parents is too difficult and skip the parent about whom you have but little knowledge. If you do decide to work with that parent, fill in the missing information using what people have told you (or what they have intimated) and what you can imagine about her/his childhood.

Now give the book to your reader or turn on your tape recording. If you have a reader, ask that person to use your mother's first name often when reading the questions to you. After you close your eyes, focus your mind and emotions intensely on the memories and imagined scenes that come to you. Ready? Begin.

EXERCISE 6: GRANDPARENTS

Pretend to be your mother when she was a child or teenager. You can skip around if you wish and be your mother at various ages, as long as you are either a child or a teen.

How do you look . . . ? What color is your hair . . . ? What is your body shape . . . ? Do you have any special feelings about your looks . . . ? Imagine yourself in the area where you live . . . . What are the surround-

ings like . . . ? Imagine yourself in your home . . . . Is it tidy . . . messy . . . ? Is it large . . . small . . . ?

See your mother [or female caregiver] come into the room . . . . How does she look . . . ? What is she like . . . ? Is she loving . . . ? Brusque . . . ? Cold . . . ? Busy . . . ? How would you describe her . . . ?

What does she do during the day . . . ? Does she take care of the house or does someone else do that . . . ? Does she cook for the family . . . ? Does she have work or activities that take her away from you and from home regularly . . . ? Do you feel you get enough of her attention . . . ? Is she intellectual . . . ? Earthy . . . ? How does it feel to be her daughter/son . . . ? Do you tell her your secrets . . . ? Do you laugh with her . . . ? Cry with her . . . ? Do you disagree with her . . . ? Openly . . . ? Silently . . . ? What does she value . . . ? Do you agree with her values . . . ?

Now think of the biggest changes that have occurred in your family life . . . . Moves to another location . . . ? Deaths . . . ? Births . . . ? Changes in family finances or social standing . . . ? Divorce . . . ? How did your mother cope with these changes . . . ? What are the most valuable things you learned from your mother . . . ? What are the things you most wanted to change about your mother . . . ? Think of anything else significant about your mother . . . .

Now, still pretending to be your mother, imagine your mother's father [or male caregiver] in your home when you were a young person. When is he there . . . ? Imagine him coming home . . . . How does he look . . . ? Hair . . . ? Build . . . ? What is your feeling when you see him . . . ? Is he warm or cold in the way he greets you . . . ? What kind of work does he do when he is away . . . ? Do you share in his work at all . . . ? Is his work intellectual or physical, or is it a combination . . . ? Are you proud of your father's work, or embarrassed, or neutral . . . ? Do you come to your father for advice or to share problems . . . ? What kind of response are you likely to get if you do . . . ? What are your father's biggest concerns or worries . . . ? Do you disagree with him . . . ? If you ever do, what is his likely reaction . . . ? What does your father value . . . ? Do you agree with his values . . . ? What have been the biggest changes in your family life . . . ? Births . . . ? Deaths . . . ? Moves . . . ? Financial changes . . . ?

*Divorces . . . ? How does your father cope with these changes . . . ? What
are the most valuable things you learn from your father . . . ? What are the
things you most want to change about your father . . . ?*

Think of anything else significant about your father . . . .

*Now, let go of the pretending. Remember the room you are in at the
moment and come back to it. Open your eyes, stretch a little, and stand up.
Take a short break.*

Next, repeat this exercise, pretending to be your father. First think
about your father's mother (or female caregiver) using the same questions,
then about your father's father (or male caregiver). The reader should ask
for the father's first name and use that name when reading the questions.

The most important purpose of this exercise is to gain more understanding and compassion for your parents. They might have done things
when you were small that you cannot honestly forgive. The initial hurt
could even have caused you to make choices you regret, so you may need
to develop compassion for yourself as well. But now you can have greater
understanding about the kind of parenting your parents received and
recognize that they were doing the best they were able to do at the time.

What remains is for you to learn any other lessons you can as a result
of having grown up in your particular family. If there were negative habits,
you can determine to stop them in your generation, so they don't hurt you
any more and so they are not passed on to the next generation . . . to your
children and perhaps their children.

Finally, as you complete the sixth exercise, think of any other people
or events that impressed you as a young person. Was there untimely death?
Were there important events involving siblings? Aunts and/or uncles?
Financial changes? Divorces? Births? How did these affect your family?
Think about the unique style of your family's reactions. Think of other
ways people react to these kinds of events and consider what makes your
family unique or special. How has this affected you and your reactions?
You may discover significant things about your family that you need to
learn more about. This may also be a good time to talk with a more

knowledgeable family member or to dig through old family records to fill in some of the gaps with regard to your roots.

SUMMARIZING WHAT YOU'VE LEARNED

You have now completed, or at least read, six exercises — Ideal Partner, Romantic Relationship History, Comparing Your Ideal Partner with Your Real Partner, Family Mobile, Remembering Childhood, and Grandparents. Now you are ready to put this material together to see a profile of your own partnership choices and the reasons or experiences behind them. This profile can be used to give you more information about how you have chosen romantic partners in the past and how you can create the kind of love you want now and in the future.

You may want to take some time to spread out all of your exercise results and look for their personal meaning to you. The information below will help you with this process.

Common Themes

The following are common themes I have observed in individuals' choices of romantic partners:

1. Choosing someone with qualities like the mom or dad who never loved or accepted you *as you would have liked*. Sometimes the person's underlying qualities are the same as those of a parent, though the form (appearance, interests, etc.) may be different. The way this person *relates to you* is most apt to be similar to the way an early caregiver related to you.

2. Choosing someone similar to a brother or sister who created an unfulfilled longing within you for acceptance, love, or equality (more about this in chapter 5).

3. Choosing someone whose problems are familiar (i.e., chemical abuse, eating problems, risk-taking, moods, etc.).

4. Choosing someone who is unavailable (i.e., already paired with someone else or geographically distant and unable or unwilling to make a change to be with you). Doing this is often a way to "correct" the loss of

a significant caregiver through death or abandonment (more about that in chapter 6).

5. Choosing someone who is the opposite of a parent with whom you had difficulty. For example, Gary's "neatnik" mother was constantly reminding him to be careful of the furniture, to wipe his feet, and to clean his room. So he carefully chose someone who was "comfortably messy." His choice was still greatly affected by his mother's behavior. Another example might be that of choosing a very gentle mate instead of one who's like a demanding parent. (However, this "gentle" person may use passive aggressiveness to dominate in another way.)

The exciting challenge of scenarios that are familiar from your childhood is that *this* time, with this new person, you can "get it right" and fulfill that old, perhaps long-buried wish. Indeed the "new" person often does provide exactly the ingredients to do just that. But your being able to choose a partner who is both able and willing to help you get it right this time requires considerable awareness of these realities on your part. And, of course, the other person has needs to be filled by you, too. More later about the exciting and challenging prospect that both of you can use your relationship to heal the past and also get present needs met. The current task is to find your own reasons for choosing who you choose — your habits of attraction.

How the Exercises May Be Used

Now compare your work with the Ideal Partner, Relationship History, and Ideal/Real Partner exercises with your Family Mobiles and the answers to the questions at the end of Remembering Childhood, then ask yourself the following questions:

1. Are the partners I have chosen most like my mother, my father, some other parenting person, or a sibling?

2. Do I see any problems I could be attempting to "get right this time" as an adult, problems over which I had no control as a child?

3. As I become more aware of my role in my original family, can I see any way I have reenacted this role in my adult life?

4. Have I re-created a mood familiar from my childhood?

As you become more aware of problematic patterns in yourself and in your family, you can choose to encourage the patterns in you that promote love and well-being and to adjust patterns that seem nonproductive or are clearly working against your best interests. In either case, the more awareness you have about the patterns you developed within your family, the more control you have over the emotions that cause you to fall in love.

Here are several examples of how others put together the results of their completed exercises and learned from them.

Jean

At forty-two, Jean has never been married. She was raised in a strict Catholic family and moved far away from them as an adult. On her Family Mobile, she described her father as a "gentle saint" and her mother as "fun" and "neurotic." When Jean looked at her Relationship History, she saw that everyone she had chosen as a romantic partner was "fun" and "neurotic." What a surprise!

The Family Rules, as she saw from her Family Mobile exercise, were strict, and Jean had consciously rebelled against them. She chose men who were "fun" and "neurotic" and also people her mother would not approve of, people she saw as somewhat dangerously exciting. To Jean, the pattern became shockingly apparent.

When she described her mother as "neurotic," Jean meant her mother was such an active participant in her church social life that she did not take care of her own personal needs. Jean's chosen "neurotics" were even more fun-loving, to the extent of being impractical and not dependable in taking care of themselves, let alone taking care of her.

"I don't want to be so influenced by my mother, yet I have been. My rebellion against those old 'rules' has caused one part of me to be attracted to men that another part of me does not approve of. No wonder relationships haven't worked for me. How can I change that?"

The first step was to recognize the problem. Jean began to see that she needed to resolve, directly with her mother, some issues she was acting out in her romantic relationships. Her answers to the questions at the end of the Remembering Childhood exercise also pinpointed her frustrations with her mother and the longings that still influenced her choice of partners. Further, she saw that men like her father seemed so safe that she felt no challenge with them, no excitement. She realized that she had focused on finding excitement but had not given any consideration at all to feeling safe and comfortable in a relationship. Perhaps she could begin to put the two together and have a relationship that was safe, supportive, *and* exciting.

Pete

Pete was married to Phyllis and struggling to decide whether he could remain in this, his second marriage.

In the Family Mobile, he described his father as "friendly" and "conservative" and his mother as "doing a good job of the role" but "impersonal," with "little intimacy." His major problem was with his mother. What Pete wanted most for someone in his family to do was to "listen to me," and what upset him most was the feeling that there was "something wrong" with him.

Pete's initial attraction to Phyllis came about because he felt she was someone he could talk to. She, like his mother, enjoyed the role of housewife and mother. After they married, however, Pete began to notice occasions when he felt Phyllis didn't really listen to him. Then he found himself looking for disagreeable ways of creating distance between them when she wanted closeness. He didn't like that in himself. It brought back the familiar childhood feeling: "There must be something wrong with me."

At the time Pete did the exercises, he and Phyllis were separated. When he saw the combined results of the exercises in front of him, he realized that what he wanted most of all in his life, and didn't have, was more intimacy. Yet that was the very thing he pushed away during his time with Phyllis.

As she began to be more her own person outside of the homemaker role, Phyllis became more attractive to him. Pete now recognized that Phyllis had the capacity to give what he needed: the ability to be intimate. He could stretch in his own capacity to be close with her, while she had already shown she could grow from increased separateness and independence (the qualities she most needed to develop). They could be wonderful teachers for each other. This recognition did not solve all their problems, but it helped Pete see the perfection of his choice and allow himself to love and grow with his wife.

Beverly

Beverly was divorced and a young grandmother. She was now a successful music teacher, using the talent and the intelligence she inherited.

Her Ideal Partner exercise showed she wanted most to be cherished and protected. This was apparent again in her answers at the end of the Remembering Childhood exercise. What she wanted most there was to be "recognized." The feelings that most upset her were "no rights," "loser," and "ugly." Part of her Family Rules were "children should be seen and not heard," "don't tell the truth about other family members if it's negative," "rich people aren't happy and don't like us," and "we pretend Dad comes first." She could see why she wanted to be cherished and protected.

On her Family Mobile she described her father as "a tyrant" and "talented." She described her mother as "intelligent" and "wasted life."

Her Relationship History revealed much to her. She saw she had chosen men who, in her eyes, were heroes who could protect and cherish her, but they eventually turned out to be disappointments, as her parents had been. Beverly saw that one man, with whom she had fallen in love most quickly and deeply, told her all the things she most wanted to hear. That realization was an important learning experience, especially since she eventually discovered he was a pathological liar!

The next man seemed to be "safer" and "cherishing." But after a while, he verbally degraded her. Beverly realized that in her attempts to be cherished, she began to take care of him and did not feel at all protected. When she realized she had been perpetuating an old pattern, she broke off the relationship.

Now Beverly can get the recognition she needs within herself, from satisfaction with her work. She has stayed out of romances for a time so she can improve her own ability to feel successful and secure. In this way she is preparing herself to recognize a healthier relationship. Her statement to me:

"My parents prepared me very well to encourage my music students. My childhood gave me such a good course in low self-esteem, I can easily relate to my students' worst feelings about themselves. I've been there! What I needed to do was turn that around and make an advantage of it in teaching my students — take the negative experience and use it. My parents have actually helped me be successful as a teacher."

Alex

Alex was fifty when he took my workshop. He had dated but never married. He envied his married friends. When he spread his Family Mobiles out in front of him, he immediately recognized the striking similarity between his mother's and father's families. The Grandparents exercise allowed him more profound experiences of these two families. Both had been dominated by the mother. Both fathers had worked hard and provided well for their wives and children. In Alex's view, neither of their marriages were happy, nor were the subsequent marriages of their children. His father and both of his grandfathers died young, their lives having had little joy or fulfillment.

Alex exclaimed, "No wonder I never married. In my family, when I was a young man, marriage didn't look very promising to me." (After the Remembering Childhood exercise, Alex wrote that what he had wanted most from his family was to feel closeness. The thing that upset him most was, "I felt alone. Dad was working and Mom was sick a lot.") Alex's relationship history showed only one romance and it was a stormy one. Since then, his relationships with women had been superficial. Group activities allowed him to be sociable without intimacy. His Partner Comparison exercise showed a wide disparity between his ideal and actual partners.

Before he did the exercises, Alex thought he simply had not met the right woman—that it was "his luck" that he hadn't married. Now he could see clear and logical reasons he had avoided marriage and not known how to achieve intimacy. With new understanding he could work on changing his patterns of behavior rather than bemoaning his luck.

At this point you have considered your own family habits from many perspectives. Your family patterns may be clear or confused. But the important thing is that you have thought about yourself in some new, focused ways. As you continue reading in this book, you can apply the insights that emerge from these exercises to your own personal situations. If problems come up that particularly bother you, you may want to discuss them with a friend, a family member, or a counselor or therapist.

Next we will focus on the circumstances of your birth and your relationships with your siblings. The entry of children into your family system inevitably created profound changes. How did your family's way of dealing with these arrivals affect who you have become and who you have chosen to be with?

5

BIRTH AND SIBLINGS
More Lessons in Loving

When your life began, your experience with the people and circumstances around you caused you to make certain decisions about "how the world is." What you may not realize is that those decisions, usually made when you were so young that you don't remember them, still have a powerful effect on your life. Therefore, reconstructing your early circumstances and becoming aware of the decisions you might have made can provide you with information that is useful today. It can have a direct effect on the romantic choices you make now, as an adult.

In fact, amazing as it may seem, certain of those decisions were made even before you were born. Technologies like fiber optics and ultrasound imaging have given researchers the opportunity to study the behavior of fetuses and their responses to various stimuli. These researchers have discovered that fetuses are very sensitive, and react to what is happening to the mother. Mother's moods cause her body to produce chemicals that she passes on to her baby through the placenta, which means that even before the baby is born, it has been significantly influenced in highly individual ways by its immediate surroundings.

When babies finally are born, the environments into which they emerge vary greatly. The physical circumstances may be anywhere from comfortable and luxurious to cramped and miserable. The emotional environment may reflect the child's being unplanned and born to parents in an uncertain relationship or its being yearned for and deeply loved by parents who are in a stable relationship. Since both physical and emotional components of the child's environment are felt by the child as similar at this point, both realities are included in a pervasive, global experience of life. In addition, the temperament the child is born with and the mood the child creates in the household are important factors as this very young person develops attitudes about self and about the comfort and safety of the world. (Of course, these aspects of the early environment may be significantly modified by later influences. For example, the unplanned child may become a blessing and be beloved. The waited-for and wanted child may be overindulged or overprotected and become problematical.)

All of these learnings about life are crucial to later choices in romantic love. In fact, the whole range of childhood experiences teaches a developing person about loving.

Calling on Exercise 5 (Remembering Childhood), try to recall your own very young childhood. What spoken or unspoken messages can you remember receiving from your parents? If your parents' messages were negative, you may have more difficulty creating a loving situation for yourself in your intimate relationships or for your child when you become a parent—and, thus, also a teacher about love.

As a partner in a romantic relationship, you may find yourself reenacting negative situations from your childhood. As a parent, you may sometimes be unable to give your children more than you received when you were little. In either case, you may come to recognize that your parents had a difficult time loving you even when they really wanted to. If this seems true for you, the first step toward correction is recognizing the problem. With understanding and determination, you can find ways to heal. (Think about how it would be for you, as a parent, to teach a child about love through your behavior. This may add some perspective to how it might have been for your parents—your teachers about love.)

One way for you to begin recognizing your early programming is to think about the answers to these questions:

1. What were the circumstances of my conception, as best I know? Were my parents married? Was I the reason for their marriage? Was my conception "accidental"? Were my parents ready for me? Were my parents unusually afraid of childbirth, of caring for a child, or of the financial responsibility?

2. What happened to my mother during her pregnancy that is likely to have affected me? Were there any deaths in the family? Did other traumatic events or circumstances occur? What were my mother's and father's attitudes about having a baby? Did they strongly prefer a boy or a girl?

3. Were there unusual circumstances about my birth? Difficulties? Was I premature?

Right now, particularly if you have recalled difficult or traumatic events, you may be asking yourself, "Well, what can I do about them now?" While you can't change the past, you can derive much value from recognizing the messages you picked up—negative or positive. You may also become aware of physical experiences you had when you were very young, or even before you were born, that could be important. With this information, you can more readily understand and forgive any upsetting attitudes you have about yourself — attitudes about being unwanted, troublesome, or unproductive; about intimacy, about the opposite sex, or about being a parent.

For example, as a small child, Deborah, whom we met in chapter 3, was told that her father sat down on the hospital steps and cried in great disappointment because she was a girl. Certainly being a girl was not anything for which Deborah could take responsibility, but her father's attitude affected her feeling about herself and contributed to her anger toward men, especially when it was strengthened by his preferential treatment of her brother.

Another example is Carla. Her parents, while her mother was pregnant with her, suffered a devastating financial setback and lost their home. At that same time, her mother's best friend died. Carla has struggled all her life with an inexplicable terror about situations that others find quite harmless. She felt something was wrong with her, until she recognized that some of her fearfulness apparently belonged originally to her mother and seems somehow to have been transmitted to her before she was born. This recognition has helped her take her fears less seriously.

The examples of Carla and Deborah suggest how a person can be affected both before and after birth by the experiences and attitudes of parents or other caregivers. Further, have you ever thought about what kinds of early messages your parents might have picked up from *their* parents, which in turn affected you? Also, your family system did not exist in a vacuum. It was a unit in a series of ever-larger social contexts (neighborhood, community, nation, world). Your family's social context also had an impact on you and affected what you learned about love. A whole encyclopedia could be written about the effects of cultural and racial influences on each of us, a subject with which we as a society are grappling more and more. It is, however, outside the scope of this book.

Temperaments

Contrary to the opinions long held by many that babies are born as "blank tablets," essentially featureless and ready to be imprinted by whatever their environment happens to present, information now available suggests that babies are already highly individual at birth.

For example, the results of thirty years of research by Stella Chess and Alexander Thomas describe substantial temperamental differences in babies. In their book *Temperament and Behavior Disorders in Children*, they describe how they observed and documented the behavior of 133 individuals from the age of three months to early adulthood. They concluded that babies are born with unique temperaments, or behavior styles, and that their individual nature has a distinct effect on the family they join.

Dr. Berry Brazelton, in his popular book *Infants and Mothers*, explores the wide ranges of babies' temperaments. Brazelton includes accounts of quiet, average, and active babies, regarding each of these different types of behavior as equally healthy and acceptable.

This research on temperamental differences points out the importance of the "fit" between the personality of the parent and that of the child. For example, a situation in which a quiet baby has fast-thinking, fast-moving, extroverted parents may require those parents to make special adjustments. Having discovered and accepted their baby's basic temperament, the parents can learn to introduce new situations to the baby more slowly, since such a baby needs familiarity to feel safe and comfortable.

Another example is that of an irritable, active, responsive baby who comes into a family accustomed to quiet and routine. This difference in temperaments may require distinctly different adjustments.

For instance, Kim lived in a reserved, intellectually oriented household in which the expression of feeling was discouraged and mental accomplishment was prized. Kim, however, was temperamentally active, noisy, and excitable from the beginning of her life. Though her intellectual accomplishments were significant, she never felt a sense of comfort or belonging in what seemed to her like a stifled family atmosphere.

We can follow this through into her romantic life to see how that conflict led to even greater problems. As an adult, she was intensely attracted to a man who was not intellectual and who expressed emotion freely. But she was not prepared for the anger that came along with other expressions of emotion. The marriage ended in a stormy divorce. Now she is trying to sort out the part of her that is temperamentally sensitive and high strung from the part that, because of her childhood environment, is afraid of emotional expression in herself and others.

A recognition that babies are born with different temperaments can help parents feel less guilt and more success when they are adjusting to this small, new human who has joined their family. Accepting that differences in temperament exist, just as differences in hair or eye color exist, can be helpful to the parents as well as to the child who has those individual traits and needs to be accepted and loved.

What kind of temperament did you have as you entered your family, and how did you affect your family? Did you fit the expectations or were you, from the beginning, somehow different? Did your temperament coincide with your parents' expectations in terms of your being a boy or a girl? Were you easygoing or were you strong-willed? How did your parents adjust to your temperament? If you do not know these things about yourself, is there someone you could ask?

BROTHERS AND SISTERS

Clearly, parents are not the only people in our families with whom we have important associations. Relationships with brothers and sisters are also powerfully influential and they often have a profound effect on how we choose intimate partners. As adults, we may yearn (usually without being aware of it) for a relationship like one with a sibling. If the relationship seemed especially good, we may idealize it and find others falling short. Or more commonly, if we longed for something from a brother or sister that we never got, we may choose partners who remind us of a sibling, with the unconscious hope that this time things will be different. "This time I'll get the love [or respect or care or attention] I always wanted from my sister [or brother]." Or: "My new lover will give me the opportunity to heal the hurt I experienced in childhood at the hands of my brother [or sister]." For example:

Ben

Ben was a new client. I asked about his childhood family. As he described his mother, absent father, and older sister, we came to see that his sister was the strong, "take charge" person in the family. Because she was older, she was given a parenting position. Mother was busy with work and activities, and the little boy became very close to his sister. She was capable but also demanding. Though Ben wanted and needed her approval, he seldom got it. He told me, "I like strong, capable women. They are the ones who attract me." But so far his romances with that type of woman hadn't worked out well.

As Ben described his recent romantic partner, Kate, he used many of the same words and phrases he used to describe his sister. Problems, he said, had emerged almost from the beginning. His performance in social and even in private situations didn't live up to her expectations. This was painfully familiar to him but also challenging, which increased his excitement and his desire to make the relationship work.

The situation was not easy but the attraction was intense, since it recaptured an emotionally charged aspect of Ben's childhood. Kate's childhood scars, however, left her with little willingness to resolve the difficulties she and Ben were having. Finally, they broke up.

Ben was sad and had a hard time letting go of his longing for Kate, though he also understood the impossibility of finding happiness with her. And he had learned something about his personal dilemma, having recognized his longing, even as an adult, to find someone like his sister who would accept him. He realized that in order for a relationship with such a woman to be successful, he would have to choose someone who had the ability to grow and heal with him.

Vera

Vera's down-to-earth parents provided constant, loving support. She could find only positive things to say about them. A bright, loving, attractive woman, Vera pondered the reasons behind her two divorces and the breakup of two other significant relationships. What came to light as we talked was that her older brother, whom she adored, had never accepted her and had been jealous and resentful of her. As a child, she tried in many ways to win his approval and love, but could not. Her relationship with her brother was the one thing from her childhood about which she did not feel successful.

She began to realize that her relationships with men re-created many of the feelings she felt with her brother. She was, as an adult, still finding men with whom she could repeat this old scene. She chose men who didn't accept her, setting up for herself the challenge to make them love her the way she always wanted her brother to love her. This provided both the exciting challenge to "get it right this time" and the seeds of her romantic failures. With an understanding of this repetitive pattern, she could begin to create relationships that had a greater chance of survival.

Birth Order

Whether you were the oldest, the youngest, in between, or an only child can have a powerful effect on the way you relate to others as an adult and how successful your romantic choices are. Imagine how different your attitudes would be had you and your siblings been born in a significantly different order.

As the oldest of three, for example, I learned to be a responsible caretaker. How would I have been different if I had been youngest instead, with people wanting to take care of me? The gender of the siblings also has an impact. The youngest sister of three older brothers grows up with very different attitudes about males than a girl who grows up as the big sister in a family of all girls. Each of these growing-up influences, of course, has a significant impact on our choices of romantic partners. Typically, the oldest is responsible and achieving, the middle is either the peacemaker or rebellious, and the youngest may expect to be taken care of or create distance to avoid engulfment. Just as temperament, gender, number of siblings, and the way we are parented contribute to forming who we are, so does birth order.

For example, the Marshall family had three boys, two years apart from one another in age. Their father worked long hours and was loyal to his family. But he did not know how to be emotionally close to his children, and his wife made up for this lack by being warm and involved in the activities of her sons.

The oldest, Ken, followed his father's example. He was a "good boy," a high achiever, responsible—and emotionally detached like his father.

Frank, the middle son, was the peacemaker. He was sensitive to his mother's needs. He was a good listener and enjoyed her attention and affection. Often he took care of his mother's feelings instead of doing what he really wanted to do. He was the "adored child" and basked in that position while also resenting the price he paid—his independence.

The youngest boy, Rob, learned to relate to his mother by opposing her and thus keeping her at a distance while still getting her attention. As the youngest, he resisted unwelcome attentiveness and control by demanding his way and becoming somewhat rigidly his own person.

This family has a theme that was carried forth quite differently by each son according to his position in the family. With mom as the family "hub," each son had a unique way to get something from her in a manner that was a function of his birth order. Dad was powerful in his example of work and silence. All of the boys became some version of their dad in avoiding intimacy. And each responded to the mother by developing his own brand of freedom vs. connection. Later, as adults, each boy created a marriage relationship consistent with his birth-order position.

According to Kevin Lemen, Ph.D., author of *The Birth Order Book*, the most difficult birth-order pairings in adult relationships are people who, as children, were the oldest in the family or were only children. Both may have the expectation of being responsible or "in charge" and be accustomed to engaging in power struggles over who is right. Two youngest children married to each other can also have difficulties, as both may expect to be taken care of. Middle children are likely to have been especially sensitive to what was happening around them when they were growing up, and also probably needed to be extra good or extra bad to get attention, to "fix" things, or to protect someone in the family. In adult relationships, they are inclined to be flexible, but can also become either overly accommodating or antagonistic.

These, obviously, are generalizations and will not always be true, as dozens of other important factors also contribute to how couples fit together. Nevertheless, this very brief explanation of sibling order offers the essence of the concept. (Dr. Lemen has written another book, *Living in a Step Family without Getting Stepped On*, about the changes that occur in sibling order in blended families.)

Other kinds of experiences in the family with siblings and, of course, with parents may cause us to make decisions early in life that, as adults, we have long forgotten. For example, "all men are . . . " or "all women are . . . " stereotyping can cause us to create the very scenario we fear.

Thus, if a woman has a view that all men are abusive because of her experience with a rageful father and/or brother, she may be attracted to men who are angry and frustrated. When she finds a man whose difficulties are familiar to her, she says to herself, "He is just misunderstood.

Underneath he is a sweet guy. I will change him." Then she is "surprised" when he turns out to be abusive, although that quality is actually (though unconsciously) what she looked for and expected—and what she got! She also may unconsciously contribute to his abusiveness by behaving toward him in an inconsistent or angry way.

Parents set the tone and limits in the family, but siblings may also be powerful teachers about what love is and is not. Becoming aware of the effects of these relationships is important, since, if what you've been choosing has not worked well for you, having this new awareness can help you choose a different behavior.

EXERCISE 7: SIBLINGS AND YOUR CHILDHOOD FAMILY

Let's focus on your life with your siblings when you were a child. Again, having someone read the exercise to you may be more effective than simply reading it yourself. But whether you or someone else reads it (or you use a tape recorder), relax and let the pictures, feelings, and voices roll over you as you go back to being a child, relating to your siblings in the "mobile" of your original family.

Pick whatever age first appears in your mind or skip around in your childhood years. If you are an only child, were other children nearby who were somewhat like siblings? If so, you may want to keep them in mind for this exercise, though the situation will obviously be different if you did not share parents.

Now, close your eyes and begin:

Do your brothers and/or sisters listen to you . . . ? To whom do you listen . . . ? Do you compete with any siblings . . . ? Who are you jealous of . . . ? Is anyone jealous of you . . . ? Who do you admire or respect . . . ? Whose approval do you want . . . ? Does anyone want your approval . . . ?

Think of difficult times for the children in your family . . . . Did you and your brothers or sisters talk with each other about your nonfamily difficulties . . . ? About troubles with your parents . . . ?

Think of the happiest times for you with your family . . . . Did these times include your siblings . . . ?

Were the children in your family each looking out for themselves or were there coalitions . . . ? Was it sometimes "the kids against the parents" . . . ? Who protected or took care of whom . . . ? Who was "the boss" . . . ? What were the most important values or purposes in your family . . . ? Did you and your siblings share these . . . ? Did you and your siblings have anything to hide . . . ? Were you and/or your siblings expected to contribute to the family in some way . . . ? Through chores . . . ? Financially . . . ? Were these responsibilities divided fairly . . . ?

When you are ready, let go of these memories and return to the room you are in. Open your eyes.

Now that you have brought siblings into the picture, you are prepared — in the remainder of this exercise — to reflect on your entire family as well as your adult relationships. Do this in whatever way is most comfortable and effective. You may want to put your reactions in writing. If you prefer, talking to someone can be useful, or you may simply wish to go over the questions in your own mind.

CHILDHOOD DRAMAS

1.   *If your family were a drama — a soap opera, a comedy, or even a tragedy — what role would you play?*

2.   *Name the other characters in your family "drama" and tell what parts they would play.*

3.   *What was the story line in your family drama? What did you keep trying to fix or wanting to fix?*

ADULT DRAMAS

1.   *How have you re-created your childhood drama in your adult romantic relationships?*

2.   *Refer to your Romantic Relationship History (Exercise 2). Look at the list of your major romances. Was your role in those relationships like or unlike your childhood role in your family? How? How did this role feel to you?*

3.   *Were there any romantic relationships in which you played a different role? How did that feel to you?*

We have considered the powerful effects of very early (and even prebirth) experiences and of brothers and sisters in contributing to your being who and what you are. These "lessons in life and love" have been powerful influences in your choices of romantic partners. They may have limited your expectations and thus limited the kinds of happiness and satisfaction you have allowed yourself. Ideally, if your relationships with siblings left you with longings for the relationship to have been different, you have found a partner with whom you can "get it right this time." You and your partner can present each other with experiences that feel better to you than past relationships felt. This is one of the greatest gifts you can give yourselves, since such experiences have the ability to heal wounds you have carried within you for a long, long time.

The next chapter will consider other kinds of hurts that you may unconsciously be trying to heal in your relationships: hurts from losses created by death or divorce in your family.

6

DEATH AND DIVORCE
Their Impact on Love

The loss of a family member through death or divorce is likely to be the most powerful event a family will experience. As such, it creates the most urgent need for revised patterns of behavior in the family system. Many other kinds of loss can occur (involving job, home, money, etc.), but death and divorce change the basic family structure and require the development of new strategies to reestablish balance. Changes in the family following a loss of such magnitude may lead to positive or negative results over time, depending on the strength, resilience, and support the family system provides and the manner in which that family system—the family "mobile"—adapts to change.

In considering the analogy of the hanging mobile, with its pieces delicately balanced to form an attractive structure, you can see how the loss of one part creates the necessity for a new kind of balance if the mobile is not to hang askew. Similarly, a major loss in a family requires that a new balance among the family members be attained if they are to adjust appropriately to the profound change that has occurred.

We will consider the impact of such a loss on you (both in your childhood and after you have become an adult) and on a child (if you are a parent or close to a child who has had a significant loss).

GRIEF

The most widespread problem that follows the loss of a family member — whether through divorce or death — is the incomplete expression of mourning, which can lead to many troublesome consequences and have a major impact on your later choice of a romantic partner. The way you experience grief can powerfully affect your personal development, your ability to be receptive to love, and your ability to give love.

Divorce

Earlier in my professional career, I worked for several years as a divorce therapist. My cotherapist, Thomas Burns, and I dealt with divorcing couples in both couples' sessions and individual sessions. He worked with the husbands and I worked with the wives. Sometimes the children were included, either with their parents or separately. We realized the importance of helping each member of the family to fully express the pain of separation and the loss of the dream of love and family. We recognized that fully experiencing each stage of the grief process (see below) was vitally important and that going beyond denial, anger, and "if only" to an emotionally vulnerable expression of sadness was essential. When the partners had uncovered their feelings of hurt and disappointment, they could heal the anger that was a defense against feeling the pain of loss.

Death

In the grief following a death, the issues are different but the process is similar. Sadness is to be expected, though anger can come uninvited and unexpectedly. The loss may have consequences that are far-reaching, even affecting later generations, and it will almost certainly affect subsequent choices of romantic partners.

We will discuss these two sources of grief and the issues they raise for each member of a family, but first we need to identify the stages of the grief process.

The Grief Process

The grief that follows any loss is a normal occurrence that includes various stages. Elisabeth Kübler-Ross, in her book *On Death and Dying*, defines them as follows:

1. *Denial* ("This can't be happening.")

2. *Anger* ("I'm angry at myself [or God, or the one who has died, or is dying, or is leaving]," or "I'm angry at the change taking place.")

3. *Bargaining, or "if only"* ("If only you won't die [or leave], I will do anything," or "If only I had not done this [or that] . . . ")

4. *Depression* ("The change is real, and I am very sad about it.")

5. *Acceptance* ("Now that I accept the change as having happened, and I have fully experienced my feelings about it, I am ready to go on with my life and do what needs to be done.")

You can recognize these stages in much simpler form in life's common mishaps, such as denting your car. First, *denial*: "What? I couldn't have done that!" Then, *anger*: "Damn it, whoever parked that other car over there was stupid!" followed by *bargaining, "if only" thoughts*: "If only I had seen it, I wouldn't have hit it!" Then *depression*: "I'm so sad my car is dented." And finally, *acceptance*: "I'd better call the insurance company and see about getting it fixed." In a minor situation, this entire process may take only a few minutes. With a major loss it can take years.

To complete a healthy grief process, expressing each of these stages is necessary. (Sometimes one or more of the stages will be experienced before the death has actually occurred or the divorce is final, especially if the event is the culmination of something anticipated over a long period of time.) If you can allow yourself to feel your emotions and express them freely, the result is a healthy recovery. If circumstances, the situations of people around you, or your own unwillingness to experience the pain cause the repression of tears or the inability to talk about or express the emotions you feel, you may get "frozen" in one phase of grief. This "freeze" can have far-reaching effects, not only because the grieving process is incomplete, but also because, when you shut down sadness and pain, other emotions such as joy and love also shut down.

Loss of a significant person, such as a parent or sibling, can be particularly difficult for a young child, because often the loss is not understood. The child, in trying to comprehend it, may reach conclusions that are erroneous. Young children are apt to feel themselves the center of their universe and think, "It's my fault that Mommy [or Daddy] went away." For a child, the grief process may also be experienced over a longer time than it is for adults, and unless the caregivers are sensitive to the child's pace, encouraging rather than discouraging expressions of grief, the child can grow up with unexpressed feelings that will affect his or her intimate adult relationships.

The child needs to tell the story over and over and talk about the person who has been lost. Drawing pictures about the experience is often helpful. If you had a significant loss as a child, consider how the adults in your life dealt with it. Did anyone help you express your denial, anger, "if only" feelings, or sadness?

As an adult, have you completed the grief you felt over major losses? Talking about the loss is important, as are crying the tears and allowing yourself to feel the stages of grief as they unfold. If friends and family tire of listening, you can write down your feelings or express them physically, perhaps by hitting a pillow or finding a private place to scream them out. Since touch is very important, having someone hold you while you cry can be wonderfully releasing.

Disorientation, the result of a shift in your identity due to the loss of a significant person, can require that you make major adjustments. One friend who was going through a divorce confided in me, "Talking to my friends is helpful, but it can be excruciatingly difficult. Each time I tell a person who didn't know about it, I feel my identity chipped away, and I have no new 'me' yet to fill that place."

Seeing the end of grief is difficult when you are in it. I asked one client going through the loss of a spouse, "Can you get even a glimpse of the light at the end of the tunnel?" She said, "Not really. But I'm glad you're telling me it's there!" Later she told me she thought of my words many times. Months went by, then she said, "The light is so beautiful when it comes. It didn't appear suddenly, but came in brief flashes at first. Gradually it was light more than it was dark, and now darkness only happens occasionally."

While loss, whether from divorce or death, leads to the same grief process, the loss is experienced differently and the needs for social support are different. Let's discuss these two major family losses separately.

Divorce: Your Own

Becoming aware of and understanding the unconscious reasons you originally chose the partner from whom you are now separating is important in being able to forgive both your soon-to-be-ex-partner and yourself. Grieving the loss of the dream you had together can also be an important part of healing.

I remember the feelings I had in going through my own divorce after a twenty-three-year marriage. The hardest thing for me to give up after having made this momentous decision was my expectation of how my life would turn out. My mourning was more for that lost identity than it was for the loss of my spouse. I knew I wanted to end the relationship, but to end the marriage was a major change!

The shift as you go from "married person" to "divorced person" can be monumental. It is as though the "map" of how your life would be lived disappears and you must start over and create a new way of living. Your involvement with basic aspects of life, such as food, housing, parenting, friendships, money, sexuality, and self-concept may be profoundly affected. To confound this challenging situation, social support for people going through a divorce, though more available now than it was for your parents and grandparents, is certainly not as easy to find as is support after loss through death (though support after a loss through death may not be easy to find, either). Referring to her suburban, "coupled" community, a client who had gone through a divorce said, "The hardest thing for me and my children to cope with has been changing our public image. We all had, at some level, bought the idea that families with a divorce were 'messed up,' and we've had to work through that with precious little social support."

The courtroom "ritual" is not like a funeral, with supportive friends and family wanting to provide comfort. In cases where the couple does not go to court, no ritual at all marks this important life transition.

As difficult as it is, however, ending a marriage can provide, after the grief, the opportunity for an exhilarating new start and the beginning of tremendous growth. Hear this statement made by a woman a year after her divorce: "I now realize that divorce, while disruptive and sad and harsh, can also open doors of aliveness and joy in ways I never dreamed possible."

Divorce: Your Parents'

Divorce is one thing for grownups. It is quite another for kids. If your parents divorced when you were young, this experience profoundly affected how you see yourself in relationship to the opposite sex. No matter how well the experience is handled, children are almost certain to have preferred the presence of two loving (and familiar) parents. But if the marriage is not healthy, ending it may well have been in the best interests of the children. Many grown-ups whose parents divorced have told me of their relief when the tension was over and their parents finally ended the marriage.

Even though divorce relieves tension, it is still a major change and a grief process is necessary. Often, however, children have difficulty feeling safe enough to express their feelings at the time of a divorce. They are aware of how fragile their parents are and they don't want to add to the problems.

As a divorce therapist I talked with many children about their parents' divorces. Here are the words of a teenager six months after his mother and father separated. I asked him how he felt at the time of the separation and how he felt when we talked.

"I didn't like it then and I like it less now. It wasn't so bad when I hoped they would get back together, but when I found out they were actually divorcing I was really mad at them. If I hadn't talked them out of it, they would have gone to separate lawyers and really made a mess of it.

"I'm going to get married for better reasons. Now I look at my parents for what not to do. I'm going to be happy in my marriage and it's going to last."

Clearly this young man was angry and he also felt some responsibility for his parents. His younger brother, twelve, had a different view. "It's better for my parents. Obviously they are happier, even though I'm unhappy about it. I think about it a lot, but it doesn't bother me as much as it used to."

If your parents divorced, what do you remember in regard to your feelings about it? Are you aware of how your feelings about this important event impacted your later choices of partners? Did you make decisions about how you expected the opposite sex to be or what kind of person was safe to marry?

For example, Jim's parents divorced when he was a young teen. His father wanted an old-fashioned woman whose interests were limited to him and their children. Jim's mother wanted children and a home, but as the children got older, she became involved in continuing her education and developed an interest in community affairs. She would be away from home several nights a week. Jim's father felt abandoned and he initiated the divorce.

Jim was disturbed about the breakup of the family he idealized but felt he could not openly grieve the loss. His mother needed him to be strong to help her through that difficult time. He was a football player and, in his view, "football players don't cry." He occasionally visited his dad and his dad's new romantic partner, but that felt strange. So he couldn't comfortably discuss his feelings about the divorce with either parent, and it wasn't something he could discuss with his buddies. He kept most of his feelings about the whole situation inside.

Years later, in his twenties, Jim fell in love with Shirley. She was focused on a home and family — exactly what Jim wanted. He wanted a woman whose interests were limited to making a home. No more divorces for him.

But after several years and two children, Jim recognized that his choice of a partner with limited interests created restrictions for him. He began to realize that he had unwittingly created a trap, something like the trap he had observed his mother in—he felt he could not freely express his own interests outside the home without inviting disapproval from his wife. As much as he had tried to avoid divorce, he sometimes thought about it.

Jim, who had not been able to grieve his parents' divorce appropriately, knew he wanted to do better than they had, to "get it right this time." But without the awareness and healing he would have gained from more fully experiencing his grief from his parents' divorce, he repeated their situation. Interestingly, Jim made his decision about whom to marry based on knowing what his father had wanted. Later in his marriage, he found himself more identified with his mother's having felt restricted.

Further information about the effects of divorce on children can be found in the book *Second Chances*, by Judith Wallerstein and Sandra Blakeslee, which reports on the authors' long-term study of the children of divorcing families. One of the most difficult situations for such children, this book notes, is that of the mother who raises the children with little financial or emotional support from the father. Even if she manages to "protect" her children from his neglect, the children's view of men and of themselves as, or with, men cannot help but be influenced. This perception is bound to have an effect on their choosing or becoming romantic partners.

For girls, father may become a romanticized figure, a Prince Charming who could make life wonderful. Or they may conclude that men are not to be trusted and, as a result, find a man who cannot be trusted.

For a boy, the deepest wound is the lack of his father's presence as a male role model and companion. The most damaged children, according to this research, were seven- to eleven-year-old boys who lost the connection with their fathers. They sometimes became protective "substitute husbands," a role inappropriate to their stage of development, or they became rebellious or rejecting, without an ally in the family.

The research on children of divorce shows clearly the importance of the continuation of healthy parenting by both father and mother. But in a deeper and more profound way, this research — by documenting the problems of children of divorce — points to a more significant issue: the importance of choosing mates well and maintaining healthy relationships. Healthy parenting is foundational to any culture, and choosing a mate well and creating a successful parenting partnership is not only important for one's personal happiness, but it is also important for each of us as parts of a healthy society. Crime, gangs, drugs, violence — all of these problems, as well as other, more subtle forms of unhappiness, though certainly influenced by a variety of societal factors, essentially begin at home, with parenting. While divorce is often the healthiest choice available for any specific couple, how much better things would be to have mother and father together, and working well together.

Stepfamilies

Thousands and thousands of adults and children are now living in stepfamilies. When going into second marriages, many adults fantasize that they will have a new nuclear family that will repair their problems and compensate for their difficult, lonely times as single parents. Childless adults going into these marriages fantasize about having a "ready-made" family and being the perfect parent for the child. These fantasies often set couples up for painful disillusionment as they discover that, in reality, rather than being one family, they are more like two factions living under the same roof. "Insiders" and "outsiders" soon emerge, for parents are torn by having to decide between loyalty to their children and to the bond with a new spouse. Children are stressed by feelings of loyalty to their biological parent in the presence of this new person in their lives. The couple, if it is to evolve and be the primary bond in the family, must often go through several steps to accomplish that task. *Becoming a Stepfamily*, by Patricia Papernow, is an excellent resource for families who are going through these phases.

Did you grow up in a stepfamily? If you did, you will recognize how the adjustments required by all members of the family colored your attitudes about the opposite sex, marriage, and your role in a family. To the extent that your family made this challenging transition satisfactorily, you probably are flexible enough to create your own happy relationship. If your stepfamily did not blend adequately, you may have scars to heal, to avoid bringing old issues into new relationships.

Death

While death always impacts families profoundly, there is a great difference between the expected loss of an aged parent and the loss of a spouse, young parent, young sibling, or child. We will focus on this latter kind of devastating loss.

Obviously, the more changes that death brings about in the lives of a family, the more profoundly the loss is felt. But the crucial factor for a family member's future emotional health (including the choice of intimate partners) is how he or she reacts to this life-changing event. If the mourning process is not complete, the individual may get stuck at one or another of the stages of grief and be unable to go on to have fully loving, healthy relationships.

For example, I know of one family in which three children in their twenties seemed to accept the death of a loved mother with stoicism — never talking about her or shedding tears over the loss. In the five years that followed, none of them married; they remained closely attached to one another. This family was "frozen" in the denial stage of grief, and they were having difficulty going on to new, loving relationships. Finally, after all of them moved into full adulthood, one persuaded the others and their father to go into family therapy. In the safety of the therapist's office, they could finally fully express their old grief. During the next year, each person's life changed, and they all began to develop healthy intimate relationships.

In another family, the reaction to a beloved mother's death was quite different. For one son, the anger resulting from the loss of the mother — who was central to the warmth of his family — caused him to focus on the flaws in his wife's intact family. He began to see problems with his in-laws that he regarded as so serious he alienated himself and his wife from them. By focusing on what he perceived as their problems, he created unhealthy ways of distracting himself from his grief. He avoided his own sad feelings and found a less threatening (though inappropriate) target for the anger he felt as a result of his mother's having abandoned him through death.

The choice of a partner following a significant loss is often an expression of the longing to replace that person. For example: Joni's father died when she was six months old. Her mother seldom mentioned her father, and she grew up feeling the incompleteness of her family. She was close to her nurturing mother but had no substitute for her father. In reflecting on her Relationship History, Joni discovered that the men in her life had all been unavailable: either married or living too far away to be accessible. These men, she realized, were her expression of longing for her father. Tearfully, she said, "It's as though if I could make one of them love me, I could change history. It would be like having my father back. To give up falling in love with unavailable men, I will have to finally accept my father's death."

Decisions about "how life is" following a severe loss through death, especially for a child, can color one's whole lifetime and even be passed on to other generations. Open discussion about the loss with adults can be helpful in correcting erroneous conclusions reached by children as they try to deal with a loss they do not understand.

Although the loss of an important person is always hard, the long-range effects are not inevitably all bad. For example, as I noted in chapter 4, my father's father died when Dad was twelve. Dad quit school and worked hard to support his mother and sisters. He was proud of this accomplishment. The legacy of pride in hard work benefited me and the next generation—my children. But other aspects of his father's death were not so beneficial, such as Dad's anger about the situation in which he found himself as a young man. These viewpoints of his affected my early choices of romantic partners, my interest in the whole subject of romance, and, perhaps indirectly, the writing of this book.

The immediate feelings of pain — of loss and grief — will always be present with the death of a loved one, but they can be handled in conscious, loving ways that leave others with good feelings instead of issues to be overcome. For example:

A Healthy Experience of Death

Carol, who was my client some years ago, had three bouts with cancer. She hoped she had conquered the illness. But one day she called me to say she had a recurrence. She wanted to work with me on unfinished emotional issues in her family. I understood that she was facing her death. In the next months, between treatments for her spreading cancer, we spent many hours together.

Carol's goal was to clear up relationships in her family in which there was anger or misunderstanding. Her mother had died when she was an infant. She had a lifelong resentment toward her stepmother and felt distanced from her father because of that. After she and I worked through some of these feelings, she invited them both to come from their home some distance away and visit her. While they were visiting, I had family sessions with Carol, her stepmother, and her father — all together — discussing the old feelings and situations that had never been talked about before. Because Carol's old grief from the loss of her mother had been expressed as anger toward her stepmother, she had not been an easy child to live with. Now, when Carol began to see herself through her stepmother's eyes, forgiveness was not far behind. She and her father became closer than either dared hope for before — bringing joy to both of them.

In sessions with her husband and children, she and the others all aired anger, opening the way to more loving relationships. They talked about Carol's impending death, and Carol explained the things she wanted done before she left her family. Carol wanted her house in order to make it less burdensome for her family to get along without her. She worked and planned to make this happen, with the help and support of her family.

In preparing for the mother's death, the family became closer. When the time came, they were ready. Her daughter was with her at home when she died, and later told me it was a beautiful experience.

At the memorial service for this determined woman, one of her children said, "She did not want her death to hurt us as she had been hurt by her own mother's death when she was a baby. She wanted us to be ready to let her go."

This family had learned important lessons about loving that they could use to create their own loving relationships in the future.

Severe losses, as we have clearly seen, can have long-range effects on families. To get a sense of how losses may have affected you, reflect on your own history (examining your Family Mobile may help stimulate memories).

- Look for severe losses and major transitions. The death of a grandparent, an aunt, an uncle, or even a close friend can be a transitional event.
- What important changes were caused by loss in your family? Was the grief from this loss expressed openly?
- Do you need to complete mourning that you did not allow yourself to feel at the time? Is there a friend or family member to whom you can talk about this? Do you need to consult a therapist, someone who is trained to deal with these specific issues? Perhaps writing about the loss or visiting the burial place of the one who died will help you complete your grief process.

PART II

MAKING OUR
RELATIONSHIPS BETTER

7

BECOMING
THE OPTIMAL PARTNER

Because family and relationship histories help you understand yourself, both are extraordinarily interesting and enlightening. But life doesn't really improve unless your behavior changes. So the issue becomes: how can you take what you've learned and put it to practical use to create the kind of loving, growing relationship you want?

In previous chapters you focused on past relationships and family. You were gathering information. This and subsequent chapters are about what you are going to do with that information. They are about you, your present, and your future. Let's start with a question.

Who are you, anyway?

- You're a "battle-scarred" adult, not in a relationship at the moment. You've experienced both joy and pain with romance. The prospect of being alone forever is scary, but so is risking the pain of loss and the dangers involved in entangling your life with another person's life. Or:
- You're in a relationship but you're not sure about it, and you wonder whether you can improve it or if it must end. Or:

- You're in a committed relationship and you want to do everything you can to enhance it. Or:
- You've never been in a serious relationship, but you want to be and are looking for help in making it happen. Or:
- You've ended a relationship painfully. You'd like to be in a new one, but you don't want to make hurtful (or even foolish) mistakes again.

In any of these cases, what can you do for yourself to feel more magnetic, scintillating, and successful and less scared? How can you become more able to attract and be attracted to the kind of partner you want — one who provides the opportunities for growth and happiness you desire? You can:

- Get to know yourself more deeply and like yourself better;
- Improve your relationship skills so you are ready, when the time comes, to make the important choice of committing to a romantic partnership;
- Take steps toward feeling more peace and contentment in yourself;
- Learn ways to be the kind of partner you'd like to have in your life.

Whether or not you are presently in a romantic relationship, you can begin right now — on your own — to identify and develop certain qualities that will make you more attractive to others as well as happier with yourself. If you now have a romantic partner, doing these things is almost certain to enhance your existing relationship. If you do not now have a romantic partner, working in these areas will contribute significantly to your being able to attract a desirable partner when you are ready for that special relationship. If you are recovering from a breakup, this time without a primary partner may be uncomfortable, but you can use it as an opportunity to reconnect to yourself.

Here are five ways you can, working on your own, improve your chances of having a good relationship. Each will be explained and amplified below.

1. *Know yourself in some new ways.*
2. *Accept and respect yourself.*
3. *Know whether you tend to take care or give care.*
4. *Know yourself as a person with many different parts.*
5. *Heal hurts from the past.*

I. Know yourself in some new ways.

The exercises in this book provide one way to recognize the major relationship habits you inherited from your unique family and relationship background. You may have tended to believe that most people feel the way you do and that your way of looking at relationships is the "ordinary" or "normal" way. But if you examine the differences between how you and others behave in relationships, you'll discover subtle facts about yourself that will be worth considering carefully. You will be able to see your own uniqueness more clearly, to know your own strengths and vulnerabilities better, and to deepen your awareness of the areas where improvement seems called for.

Knowing yourself well enough to recognize your "sore places" from the past is important in relationships. If a situation with a partner triggers feelings from a past hurt, you can recognize them as such and be clear with your partner that he/she is getting the "bill" from a past deficit. You can be clear that although your feelings are genuine and they were triggered by the present circumstance, the depth of your feelings was *not* caused by the present circumstance with your partner. This kind of conscious awareness comes from knowing yourself and accepting your own hurt, vulnerable places.

For example, Eileen's childhood was affected by her parents' financial struggle as she was growing up. Her marriage to a man from a poor family who became successful ended in a divorce, one which was made more painful by arguments over money. In her second marriage she recognized that she still carried old feelings — deficits with regard to matters about trust and money. When these feelings came up, instead of blaming her new husband, she told him of her painful past experiences and vulnerability. Together they worked out a way for her to feel safe and to begin building feelings of trust.

2. Accept and respect yourself.

In thinking of myself as an individual, I am reminded of many techniques I have learned to help me "love myself better." But no matter how much I practice them — whether they are self-esteem exercises, affirmations, motivational tapes, or inspiring video cassettes—*I don't feel much better about myself unless I actually change my behavior and begin to take some of the actions I have decided are important.*

You may have some of these same feelings when you hear talk of "loving yourself." You may also have the nagging feeling that loving yourself is fine, but that the love you desire should occur between two people, not just with yourself. You know from your earliest, most primitive memories that you needed others, your parents, to survive when you were very young. Emotionally you still want to receive love from others and give it in return. Nevertheless, accepting *yourself*, respecting *yourself*, liking *yourself*, and being comfortable with *yourself* is also very important. This acceptance, respect, and comfort include feeling you have enough worth to be good to yourself, to be your most attractive, and to be as healthy as possible.

One way I know I am liking myself is by noticing how comfortable I feel when I'm alone and thinking my own thoughts, without attention-grabbing distractions such as TV or snacking. How content I can be by myself is one gauge of my inner sense of self-worth. If I am not able to feel good by myself, I need to take a deeper look inside, to find what I want that I am looking for others to supply.

One thing that may get in the way of your feeling good about yourself is disappointment associated with a broken relationship. If that is holding you back, you can give yourself credit for having attempted — through your choice to be with that person — to grow. Perhaps you can say something to yourself like, "In relationships there are no mistakes, only lessons." If you are still blaming the ex-lover for making you miserable, see if you can reclaim your own power. Do not continue to give that person (or any person) the power to make you angry or unhappy, even if you are still grieving the loss. Recognize the power of your own courageous choice in having attempted to heal something difficult in yourself by choosing that person. Even if it did not work out the way you hoped, it was your sincere attempt at growth and happiness. You can learn from the experience and have renewed respect for yourself.

This is something I had to come to terms with after my second marriage ended. I remember the sense of power I had when I finally reached a place where I knew that no matter what my former husband did or did not do, his behavior was not going to determine whether I was happy. Here are some of the questions I asked myself at that time, questions similar to those you may want to ask yourself:

What caused my relationship to go awry? Was the initial challenge or excitement connected with a feeling I always longed to have from my father or mother? Was I disappointed in this romance because I was not loved in the way I always wanted to be loved? Did I choose someone with whom I re-created the same old scenario from my childhood — one that caused me pain and that I hoped to heal?

Going through this process of self-acceptance was very important in my preparing for, or even being able to open myself to, another romance. My answers to those questions caused me to recognize how much I was motivated by a desire to heal old hurts from childhood, and they also caused me to give myself credit for my attempt.

Accepting yourself, however good or bad your history may be, is of primary importance in your being able to love another. And whatever you can do to support good feelings about yourself will help. Sometimes developing a new interest, skill, or goal can be helpful. For example, you might learn to play a musical instrument, plant flowers, or be more eventempered with people around you. You might learn to make yourself more attractive, get in shape, or cook better food for yourself.

3. **Know whether you tend to take care or give care.**

This is an important refinement in knowing yourself. All of us, when we are little, recognize that our survival depends on the big people who care for us. But if we sense neediness in our caregivers (they want *us* to care for *them*), we may, even as little children, feel compelled to give them that care so we can be assured of our own survival.

The ways children care for their parents vary greatly. Children may be obvious in their caretaking by being super-good or not so obvious by being super-bad (and thus distracting their parents from a painful marriage). The super-good child may help with housework without being asked or stay out of the way or provide empathic listening the parents are not getting from each other. If there is an unfilled need in parents, at least one child in the family will usually attempt to fill that void. This is an illustration of the family system, or family mobile, in operation—always attempting to maintain its inherent balance or design.

Do you recognize this kind of pull toward a particular norm in your family? Did you or someone else in your family pay a price to maintain the status quo? Such a way of reacting may become a pattern that carries over to intimate adult relationships. If this is the case, you may habitually submerge your own individual needs until you actually forget what they are. That can make it truly difficult for you to be honest about what you want in your relationships with others.

Were either or both of your parents needy, wanting you to take care of them in some way? Do you now choose people who need you to take care of them? Perhaps you have a habit of doing what the other person wants at the expense of your own wishes, hopes, and dreams. What does your Relationship History tell you about this?

Or do you look for someone to take care of you? This may not be so obvious and it may be very hard to admit, especially if you regard yourself as a "big, strong man" or a "liberated, self-sufficient woman." If it's there, your Relationship History may help you see it.

The ideal in an equal relationship (the only kind that will work in contemporary times!) is to have mutual nurturing. Nurturing cannot be bought with money. It is demonstrated through caring acts. While this may actually translate into one partner's providing monetary security for the other, the rigid old days when the man was inevitably the money earner and the woman was inevitably the sole caregiver are over, with more equality in both roles becoming the norm.

Where are you on this continuum between taking care and giving care? Do you need to learn to nurture yourself more or to enjoy nurturing others more?

4. Know yourself as a person with many different parts.

Inside of us are many parts, or voices — sometimes called "sub-personalities" — wanting to be heard. Often in our conversation we may say, "A part of me feels happy [or sad or uncaring, etc.]," while, at the same time, we recognize another part that may be saying something entirely different. Often we are not fully aware of the struggles going on inside. Our Inner Critic may say, "Get yourself in shape. You know you need more exercise and less rich food!" But the Inner Child may say, "I'm tired and I deserve that last piece of cake." Thus: conflict. Two other voices commonly in conflict are the Pusher and the Player. Example: the Pusher says, "You should meet your deadline to get that job done," and the Player says, "You deserve some time to relax and have some fun."

None of these parts or voices is inherently either good or bad, and they all serve a purpose in taking care of you. They are like the musicians in an orchestra, and you can consider yourself the Conductor, striving for balance and harmony. But if one musician plays too loudly or too long, the music suffers. Likewise, if one part of you is too much in control or overwhelms the other parts, your life does not have balance and harmony. Also, Pusher and Critic may team up to make you a workaholic or a perfectionist. Or if Inner Child and Player are in control too often, you may not accomplish your goals.

You can find your own names for the inner voices that show up from time to time. They all intend to support you in some way but may get out of harmony if you, as Conductor, do not keep order.

Creating harmony among the parts of yourself is also helpful so you will not feel complete confusion when your orchestra of parts comes together with another orchestra — in a partner. Certainly you can get knocked off balance at times, but if you discover repeated episodes of painful or unproductive disharmony in yourself, you will want to address the problem now, in order to be ready for a successful romantic relationship or to enhance your current relationship by catching potential problems before they erupt into real difficulties. Later in this book, you will find suggestions for getting help with these kinds of dilemmas. Three books by Hal and Sidra Stone—*Embracing Our Selves, Embracing Each Other*, and *Embracing Your Inner Critic*—further describe how we can use knowledge of our subpersonalities in getting to know ourselves and also in relating more successfully to others.

5.   Heal hurts from the past.

Healing old hurts is a most important ingredient in having a successful intimate relationship. If you see (from your Relationship History and your Family Mobile exercise) that the same old issues keep tripping you up and you are discouraged about relationships ("There is no one out there for me!" or "Why can't I get along with this man [or woman]?"), you may need to consider putting forth serious individual effort to deal with the issues — the baggage — you have collected that cause your difficulties. Much of this kind of baggage is likely to be outside of your awareness and to remain there unless you do some conscious inner work on yourself.

Being aware of your problem issues is a crucial first step in healing, since a lack of awareness of your own attitudes is like viewing the world with blinders on. For instance, your feelings about the opposite sex are caused largely by your past experiences, which can lead you to feel like a victim and to blame others rather than seeing your problems as something over which you have control.

Identify your major emotional traps (the exercises in this book can help you do that). What one pattern or quality has created the most pain in your relationships? For example, a client said to me, "My mother was critical and I could never be quite good enough. So I've chosen partners, without even being aware of it, who helped me recapture that old, familiar, uncomfortable feeling." Experiencing an exciting and challenging relationship without this comfortable old trap would provide a wonderful release. Thus, to recognize the trap is to take the first step toward something new and better.

Also, be aware that expectations from your past may cause you to sabotage relationships. If you catch yourself thinking "All men are . . . " or "All women are . . . ," look deep inside yourself to see how that expectation causes you to behave so as to create the very kind of relationship you fear.

This sort of insight takes self-honesty and courage, for changing or healing yourself is not easy. But it is most rewarding work, and doing it is certainly easier than trying to change others to fit your expectations.

The five areas you have just explored deal with self-knowledge and involve working on your own. Here now are four more important areas. They involve enhancing your relationship abilities by working with and experiencing others.

1. *Communicate your feelings honestly and directly.*
2. *Really listen to others.*
3. *Have high-quality same-sex friendships.*
4. *Choose people and situations carefully.*

I. Communicate your feelings honestly and directly.

If you know and accept yourself, you can more easily express your real feelings to others rather than blaming, complaining, placating, or preaching, or just ignoring the feelings. A most important relationship skill to learn is that of communicating your feelings, wants, or needs directly, by beginning your statements about what is happening inside you with the words, "I feel . . . " or "I want . . . . " This is called an "I" message. It is a very powerful communication tool that conveys to partners exactly what's happening to you without putting any blame or responsibility on them. (It will work wonders with everyone else, too.) It's worth practicing!

This kind of communication is most powerful when you have a definite feeling about something and you are willing to be responsible for that feeling. For example: "I feel unimportant to you when you are late, and that, in turn, makes me feel sad." If you catch yourself making feeling statements starting with "you" ("You make me feel upset when you are late."), recognize that you are throwing the other person on the defensive with your implications of blame. See if you can learn to take responsibility for your own feelings by starting with "I" and then reporting those feelings in detail.

Another benefit of direct communication is that you do not charge your partner with the task of figuring out what's going on in you. Expecting others to read your mind is not fair ("If he [or she] really loved me, he'd [she'd] know what I want."). No matter how well you know another, *you* still must say how you feel and what you want. Example: "I get really frightened when you are late if I don't know why you're late. I'm afraid something bad has happened to you. I care about you and it would be terrible if you were in an accident." That is much easier for another to respond to than a blaming or complaining statement ("You thoughtless jerk, you're late again!"), yet you are expressing the depth of your feeling rather than pretending everything's okay or ignoring the lateness.

In learning to present "I" messages, notice when you hear yourself complaining and notice what you are complaining about. Then turn the complaint around, into a positive request. If you notice you often use the words "always" and "never" in your complaints, recognize that these may reflect infantile viewpoints, appropriate to an earlier time in your life. (Children think in terms of extremes and most of us tend to do likewise under pressure.)

Wishes phrased in always/never ways are difficult for others to respond to. "You never take the trash out" is probably not a true statement and will not elicit understanding from your partner. When you recognize your "always" and "never" inclinations, you might change "You never give me a real kiss when you leave" into "I really appreciate it when you give me a good hug and kiss before you leave." Another example: "You always make demands on my time" could become "I need at least thirty minutes a day totally alone."

First knowing your own individual needs and then communicating them positively and specifically can provide appropriate relationship limits and guidelines. It also helps you be known by the other person. This skill can be practiced with friends and colleagues as well as with a romantic partner.

2. Really listen to others.

This is a useful skill whether you're in an intimate partnership or not. Really listening (sometimes referred to as reflective or empathic listening) is one of the best gifts you can give another person. This kind of listening requires setting aside your own agenda for the moment and listening not only to the words but also to the feelings behind the words. The more intimate the relationship, the more important it is to listen for the feelings and be able to reflect them back to the one you care about, so that person knows you hear and understand what has been said. If you wrongly understand the feelings, the other person will know immediately and tell you so, and the meaning can then be clarified. For example (in answer to the above "I" statement about lateness): "When I'm late and you don't know why, you're scared that something bad happened to me, right?"

After the fear and upset have been heard and understood, the explanation can also be heard and understood — perhaps in the form of another "I" statement, such as, "I've been stuck in traffic and feel really frustrated that I couldn't get here on time." The response might be, "Oh, so being late is frustrating to you, too."

What could have been an argument full of blaming (or swallowed feelings that are left to come out later) is over, cleared up in moments. This is a simple example of a most powerful romantic skill, and one worth cultivating. A side benefit is more progress in knowing yourself and your partner. This skill can also be practiced with friends and colleagues.

3. Have high-quality same-sex friendships.

Having same-sex friends is an important way to be understood, to feel supported, and simply to enjoy fun and companionship, so you are less dependent on your intimate relationship. Also, such friends give you more opportunities to practice saying directly what you want and really hearing what others are saying and feeling.

The differences between men and women show up decidedly in same-sex friendships. From their childhood, women have been taught that showing vulnerability and being open with one another is okay. Men learn not to show vulnerability in order to protect themselves from hurtful criticism and to enhance their ability to be competitive with one another. Because of these differences, women can typically share intimately together with greater ease, whereas men are apt to share more superficially, often having discussions that are limited to sports or work.

Women tend to solve problems by talking them through, coming to conclusions as they talk. This may drive a problem-solving, goal-oriented, "what's the bottom line?" type of man to frustration. Women (and some men) usually know when friends simply want a listener, not advice about how to solve the problem. This is one reason that, for most women, having friendships with other women is important, if not essential, for a well-balanced life.

Large numbers of men in our culture have been shortchanged in their opportunities to express feelings and be vulnerable. Many, however, are beginning to want freedom from this stereotype. For example, greater numbers of young fathers are closer to their children. They want not only to know their children better but they also want to learn about their own feelings and be freer to express themselves.

Major changes are going on collectively for both men and women, though the men's movement (which these days seems to have lost some of its momentum) is not like the women's movement. The women's movement, which has been and still is "outward" and political, was set in motion by centuries of repression. By contrast, the men's movement is largely "inward," dealing with expanded sensitivity to emotion, vulnerability, and relatedness.

A newer development for both men and women involves a groundswell of interest in reconnection with the "soul" part of individuals. It is an inner longing—a personal journey, not a political one. For women, the best-selling book *Women Who Run with the Wolves*, by Clarissa Pinkola

Estes, Ph.D., is an expression of women's search for their true nature and feminine essence. Estes writes, "Within every woman there is a wild and natural creature, a powerful force, filled with good instincts, passionate creativity, and ageless knowing . . . . Society's attempt to 'civilize' us into rigid roles has plundered this treasure, and muffled the deep, life-giving messages of our own souls." The positive response of women to this book is intriguing. But I am puzzled that a similar kind of longing, expressed in the men's movement, has generally been maligned by the press, especially by women.

As a therapist I have heard over and over a deep longing *from women* for their men to be more in touch with their own inner life. There is a great loneliness that women talk to one another (and their therapists) about — a longing for deeper sharing with men and a despair at the old resistance of men to knowing themselves in a way their partners can share deeply. But when men *do* attempt to connect to their feelings as males, some of these same women feel threatened, and that's puzzling to me.

The men's movement comprises many different subgroups. Perhaps the most thoughtful and hardest to define among its segments is the "mythopoetic" subgroup, whose focus parallels women's search for soul. It is not political as the feminist movement is. Rather, it is intended to help men facilitate the inward search and a connection with their intuitive, free, creative maleness — their soul-self.

Another subgroup consists of members of twelve-step programs, whose purpose is to support one another in overcoming addictions and in anger management.

Among events that could be regarded as part of the men's movement was the Million Man March in Washington, D.C. in October 1995. It had a decidedly spiritual meaning for many participants. Also, there have been "Promise Keepers" meetings in cities throughout the country. These meetings, which have attracted thousands of men, support traditional family values, such as responsibility and faithfulness.

Some of the books being read by men (besides the best-selling *Iron John,* by Robert Bly) include *King, Warrior, Magician, Lover*, by Robert Moore and Douglas Gillette and *Knights without Armor,* by Aaron Kipnis.

Moore and Gillette argue convincingly that "mature masculinity is not abusive, domineering or grandiose, but generative, creative, and empowering to self and others." Male readers are being specifically targeted by many other writers. In addition, small local groups of men are meeting to talk about their lives in meaningful ways.

Though women's groups have been around for a long time, I see the current tendency among both men and women as something new, a positive step toward overcoming loneliness and fulfilling the longing in both sexes for deeper meaning and connection. I think few people — women or men — really understand the emotional constrictions men have had to live with as they sought to support and maintain the power-oriented disposition they inherited.

My husband, for example, shared with me the following excerpt from his personal journal, which was written a short time before we met:

> Something in me must have recognized that all was not well — I remember feeling resentful of both my wife and my daughter for their "lack of respect" for me and how I felt at the periphery in matters that were crucial to the satisfactory conduct of my life—this "lack of respect" and the responding pattern of my behavior started in relationship to my mother and continued throughout my marriage—I remember feeling "not in charge" of my life at many moments and wondering what that was about, having a sense of not being able to get underneath the many conflicting currents of my life to a broader understanding/perspective of what it meant. I see now that what was showing up was my immaturity—that I simply had failed to grow in self-awareness as an adult. Finally, my wife became so disenchanted with what she saw as my self-centeredness that even she decided my liabilities as a life-partner outweighed my assets.

> I had been getting all my material needs met and physical needs (exercise) and interests (sports) satisfied — but where I completely fell short was in my emotional growth. I was stunted—an emotional "pygmy." Yes, I thought I was pretty happy with it, too. My belief was that this situation was a STRENGTH! This belief enabled me to feel untouched or unaffected by others—that I was able to "tough out" life.

> The apex of success was not being emotionally caught up in any of the highs and lows of daily living. I relished the ability to flaunt my insensitivity. The "ideal" man was above showing vulnerability. That

conveyed weakness, insecurity, anxiety, loss of control. My mind, my rationality—that's all that really counted—any of this emotional stuff was ultimately weakness.

I honed this capacity as a means of feeling good about myself. The more self-sufficient I could become, and the less emotionally susceptible I became, the more protected I felt against the exigencies of life. That is just the way my dad was—he modeled it as an effective way of being— The growing-up messages I got from him were: self-sufficiency is prized, even at the expense of loneliness and isolation — they were simply necessary costs of being invulnerable—and invulnerability was the key to successful, non-upsetting, comfortable, secure, and satisfactory living.

I had made an unconscious contract with myself I no longer wanted to keep. To keep pain and hurt at a minimum, I also kept joy and aliveness at a minimum. Intimacy was impossible. I no longer wanted to settle for that. With the help and encouragement I got from other men on my path, I have, over time, changed my life experience from drab shades of gray to exciting TECHNICOLOR! It has been a fascinating and worthwhile journey, complete with its roller coaster of feelings.

This kind of experience for men is becoming more widespread, and lucky am I to relate to a man who has grown in this way. If you are a man wanting the best in a relationship with a woman, I recommend such a journey beyond the traditional male role for getting to know yourself. There are men's centers and men's groups in many cities and communities, and there are also periodic conferences and regional workshops for men. I am aware of two major cities — Austin, Texas, and Seattle, Washington — from which publications originate that focus on men's issues. In the bibliography, I have listed several books written by men who are discovering how to be more truly themselves.

4. Choose people and situations carefully.

Consciously choose to be with people who are emotionally healthy and growth-oriented. Recognize the trap: "I will love him [or her] so much that he [or she] is bound to change." We can change as a result of a relationship, but are not likely to do so according to another's formula. Would you want a partner's major goal for you to be a hope that you would change? Probably not. However, the outwardly stated mutual purpose of supporting each other's wants, needs, and growth is healthy and quite unlike having a secret agenda that includes the desire for another to be different.

I remember hoping my former husband would change in certain ways. My silent manipulation, even though I thought it was loving, never made my hoped-for changes happen. But it certainly did damage the quality of our relationship. Now if there is a change either my husband or I wants, we say so explicitly and then we negotiate. Often we both learn and grow from this interchange. That feels more honest than my former way of silently hoping my partner will somehow become different.

If you are single and looking for a relationship, carefully choose the situations you put yourself into. Take risks with new situations, but be sure they are wholesome ones, in which you are likely to meet the kinds of people you want to be with. Stretch your limits and go to new and interesting places. When I was single I was not always brave enough to go places I had not been before, so I fortified myself with a "buddy" to do these things. Or I sometimes went to familiar places alone.

Even though joining new groups of people can be challenging, I strongly recommend it. Get involved in some social, educational, or sporting activities that are a little uncomfortable because they are new, but that are also a stretch in the direction of growth. Of course, some of these things may turn out not to be right for you, but you won't know that for sure until you experiment.

EXERCISE 8: EXPLORE YOUR VALUES AND DREAMS

"Who am I?" "Where is my life going?" Examining and responding to these kinds of questions is a significant aspect of the inner search — an aspect that is required for you to know yourself better. It is important preparation for communicating with a partner, as well as for knowing yourself.

The following questions have helped me to clarify my own direction and may be useful for you. (Note that I find this exercise is best done alone and in writing, though it can be done aloud with a friend.)

1. What has been important to me at various stages in my past? What do I see as "mattering" or concerning me in the future? How is my life focused now? How long will this remain so?

2. What sort of training or learning have I had? How useful is this to me now? What training or learning would I like to have in the future?

3. What sort of person do I want to be in one year, five years, ten years, or twenty years? What shifts in myself and in the use of my time must I make to achieve this? What can I do this week to begin?

4. When I am very elderly and look back at my life, what will I regret and with what will I be inwardly content?

After you have finished considering these questions, look again at your answers to the Ideal Partner exercise. Examine each item and decide whether it really is a priority for you, given your own life goals. If you want to, you can change your list.

Are you satisfied with your own progress toward becoming the kind of partner you want to have? How would it be to live with someone like yourself? What would you like to do to improve your desirability to the partner you love or to a person you would like to attract?

8

ARE YOU
READY, WILLING, AND ABLE?

The common lament of single people is, "How do I meet someone right for me?" As I see it, though, other issues must be addressed first. They involve questions of *readiness* and *willingness*: "Am I somehow sabotaging my chances of partnering without realizing I am doing so?" and "Am I doing a good job of getting to know the potential partners I meet?"

Actually finding people to get to know is a secondary matter, though it can be tough these days. For many generations, it was handled through traditional social events. But in today's increasingly rootless and highly mobile society, many of those time-honored ways of connecting have lost their relevance. More people are single than ever before. Shifting values have confused what used to be the fundamental, unwritten codes that guided meeting and being together. In urban centers, most people are strangers to one another.

Hundreds of singles clubs and dating services have sprung up around the country to deal with these changing circumstances. Nevertheless, as a culture, we are still, in my opinion, not doing a good job with what has become a major problem: the need of people to meet appropriate possible partners under circumstances that are comfortable for them and that allow them to get to know one another in more than superficial ways. Later we

107

will look more closely at this matter and discuss specific ways to meet potential romantic partners. But for now, let's examine the question that really needs to be answered first: "Am I ready and willing?"

Self-Sabotage

Meeting new partners? You've tried. You've done it. You've polished your skills, met dozens of new people, made all the right moves. And yet you're still sleeping alone, shopping for one, talking to your mirror instead of to a partner. Your television is the most significant part of your social life. Your biological clock is not just ticking, its alarm is waking you up at night. You're just downright lonesome. What, you wonder, are you doing wrong?

It's time to consider that you are, and maybe always have been, your own worst enemy. It's time to consider that you may be involved in self-sabotage. Here are two tough but important questions you can ask yourself:

Do I Really Want an Intimate Relationship?

At first, you may answer "of course." But let's look at the costs of being in a relationship. To choose anything, we are forced simultaneously to eliminate other possible choices. As long as we don't choose, we can fantasize about all of them. Men often dream about the "perfect" woman —blonde, curvy, long-legged, bright, funny. A woman is likely to hold out for rich, handsome, cosmopolitan, athletic, debonair. Your personal fantasies may be very different from these stereotypes, but nevertheless, as soon as you commit to one person, all the others, along with their wondrous fantasy qualities, become unavailable. (Even if you are now with a partner, you may find yourself refusing to commit to your relationship because of a hope that someone better will come along.)

Imagine that the last evening of a special vacation trip has arrived. You know you may never return to this place. You are hungry and in a wonderful restaurant. The menu has so many delicious items that choosing just one seems impossible. But if you don't choose *something* you cannot have the full experience of dining. The hardest part of making a choice is to give up all those other "dishes." But unless you do, you may never have the meal at all!

If you don't avoid relationships because you fear giving up your dreams of "perfection," you may avoid them because you fear the hurt that could come if you eventually break up. Or your shyness or lack of confidence may keep you in the relative comfort of being alone. If one of these is the case, you may well have unconsciously set your standards so narrowly that you can pretend to look and continue to fantasize, but not really be available.

How Could I Be Sabotaging My Relationships?

Learning about your hidden patterns may help you discover what keeps you from getting what you say you need and want, and it may also reveal what you do to get in your own way. Here, for example, are two instances of how unwitting sabotage was discovered:

When David finished the Family Mobile — a picture of three generations of his family — he said, "No wonder I'm fifty and have never married. Marriage looks pretty grim for the men in my family." David saw how family patterns produced fears that led him to sabotage his chances for a satisfying relationship. What he saw was that both of his grandmothers had dominated their families. Both grandfathers had worked hard to support their families successfully, and both died young. David's mother, because of the stress in her family, had psychosomatic illness when David was a child. His father had to take on home responsibilities as well as work very hard to support his family. He also died young. From David's perspective, no one in his family had a satisfying marriage.

Although his purpose in taking my workshop was to learn how to find a marriage partner, David quickly realized that he had other issues to resolve first. He saw that negative messages about marriage he picked up from his family, though "forgotten," were still operating outside of his conscious awareness. They were a major cause of his having sabotaged efforts to create a committed relationship. David's problem was not that he didn't know how to find partners; it was that one aspect of him didn't really *want* a partner. He realized he would have to work first at changing his psychological programming if he was going to bring marriage into his life.

Pete is another example of someone sabotaging relationship success. A salesman, Pete often attended parties where making a good impression was important, so he wanted a woman who "looked good" and was fun in these social situations. His top priority for an ideal partner was that she be beautiful and glamorous. However, his relationship history with this kind of woman indicated a series of relatively shallow and short involvements.

After completing the exercise in chapter 7 — "Explore Your Values and Dreams"—he saw clearly, and somewhat to his surprise, that what he wanted most in his life was not glamour, but a family. When he imagined himself as elderly, looking back over his life, he saw grandchildren around him. And after recognizing that he was sabotaging what he really wanted by choosing inappropriate kinds of women to spend time with, he began to change his criteria. He looked for a woman who would make a good mother and life companion. He still sought out attractive women, but he began to regard them differently. One result of his new perspective was that he began treating the women in his life as equals rather than "objects," so the quality of his relationships changed, becoming deeper and more satisfying.

David's and Pete's stories are examples of how people often keep themselves from intimate relationships without realizing it. Does part of you need protection against the fear and risk involved in a committed relationship? Are you afraid of re-creating a difficult, early-family situation in your own life? Were you emotionally or physically abused or molested as a child, or did you have other experiences with sex or intimacy that caused you pain?

You can protect yourself from the risk (and satisfaction) of romantic involvement in many ways. Common ones include deliberately being less attractive than you know you can be, becoming overweight, being critical of everyone you meet, being overanxious or clingy, not staying with anyone long enough to get close, or distancing by demanding "space" or more time. The list of such tactics is long and any of them may be perfectly appropriate or understandable in a given situation. But if you see the emergence of a consistent relationship-destroying pattern that includes these behaviors *and yet you still want a relationship*, you may be sabotaging yourself without realizing you are doing so.

This is an area where more than one inner voice, or subpersonality, is commonly heard. For example, a particular voice complains: "I'm so lonely! I want a romance so much! Why are my friends together in couples and I'm still alone? There just aren't any good partners left. I feel hopeless about finding someone even though I try so hard." But another voice inside (perhaps covertly) is saying something like, "Are you kidding? I'm not going to risk the pain and limitations I've suffered from being close to another person. Sure it sounds nice to have a partner, but it's just too risky, too frightening. I may look, but I'm not getting trapped again. It's a lot easier to be alone." These viewpoints of the various inner voices should not be taken lightly, as some or all of them may be well-grounded. They may be signaling you to do some work to heal old wounds before you undertake a serious new relationship.

BUT SUPPOSE YOU MEET SOMEONE
YOU REALLY DO WANT TO BE WITH

Getting to Know This New Person . . . Effectively

After you have met someone you would like to know better, how can you best get to know him or her? Choose activities for mutual participation that provide realistic opportunities to become better acquainted. A long walk makes possible the opportunity to talk. Going out to dinner is expensive, though it offers more time to visit than does a play or movie. If the potential new friend is not interested enough to do something simple and inexpensive, perhaps this answers one of the major questions in your screening process.

Any kind of important decision-making involves many possibilities. (Much unconscious data has gone into your head, heart, and body about romantic possibilities.) Your Ideal Partner list, which may be updated and amplified as you learn about yourself and others, can help you sort out what is really important to you. If you are genuinely attracted to someone who does not match what your list describes, ask yourself what reasons you have for being attracted to that person now. Perhaps the reasons have to do with your original family. Or your list may not be realistic.

Truly taking the time to get to know a potential partner is extremely important. We all try to put our best foot forward with a new person we want to impress, and a potential partner will, of course, do the same. But we need to be careful that, as the relationship develops, we're dealing with reality and not just images and smokescreens.

How can you enlarge your understanding of a new person? Meeting each other's family and friends is an excellent way to deepen your mutual knowledge. From your exploration of your family system and your Relationship History, you will be sensitized to the history of the people you meet. How does this person feel about his/her mother and father? Were there significant hurts or losses? Were siblings a joy or a problem? (All of us have some problems in our past, but most important is our attitude with regard to learning from mistakes, being optimistic, and having a willingness to change and grow.)

What expectations of love and family has this person developed from his/her life-experience? And what can you learn about your new friend's relationship history? This kind of information should not be hard to discover, since most of us like to talk about ourselves to someone who is genuinely interested. Give close and thoughtful attention to asking good questions and *really listen to the answers.* Pay attention to the person's past efforts to learn from misfortune. Be specific in your "interviewing" and observations. For example: if addictions have been a problem in your family, give attention to how this new person reacts to a stressful situation. More drinks? More work? Withdrawal? Exercise? Talking (to you or others) about the causes of stress? What additional ways?

Revealing yourself is the other side of "interviewing" another. While "confessing" your faults and past problems on a first date, or even a third, is not necessary, you can obviously be more open about yourself as your interest deepens. Healthy intimacy is built on honesty, not pretense. If you are open about sharing your own life, the other person will probably also be open.

How Do You Meet Prospective Partners?

It is fundamental to the ongoing quality of family life that we choose to couple wisely; the choice of a mate is among the most important of our lifetime. Yet collectively, our methods for doing this are, for the most part, extremely haphazard. Especially in big cities, while there are many ways to meet prospective partners, the settings often do not assure personal comfort, and people cannot behave genuinely enough to become acquainted with one another.

One client, an attractive woman in her late forties who had been divorced for over a year, shared this experience of a singles event:

> The object is to meet as many people of the opposite sex as possible. I walk into the restaurant advertised for this event. I sign in, pay the fee, get a name tag. That's the easy part. Then I look over the scene. There are plenty of men. The long room is crowded and noisy with dance music and the conversation of people trying to be heard over the din.
>
> Let's see, get something to drink and something to munch. Armed with what I hope is a pleasantly purposeful expression I go toward the bar, past expectant faces, busy hands, and nervous feet. I look at everyone male, while pretending not to. I'm on the older side of young, so I skip the very young ones.
>
> Most people haven't paired off yet. I get a soft drink. No alcohol. I need all my senses. I get some pieces of raw zucchini and carrots and some runny dip on a paper plate. It all tastes alike—and hits my stomach like it doesn't belong there. Now, what next? I look around, fervently wishing a man would come up to me to alleviate the tension of standing alone in the midst of all these people, most of whom seem to be talking to someone. I say to myself, "Now just take a breath and look at the situation. You're an intelligent, attractive woman. Who would you like to meet and how can you start a conversation?"
>
> I look around. I don't feel better. There's a woman near me who appears friendly. I talk to her. That's better. I'm talking to *somebody*. She tells me about other singles groups. After a few minutes the butterflies in

my stomach begin to diminish and I think, "This isn't why I'm here. Better get on with it."

While the woman talks, my eyes take in the men. I see a few possibilities. My new friend and I part with unspoken understanding. Off on my own, I see a man who looks interesting and so head for the dance floor behind him. Just as I get near the floor, a cute young female comes up to him and he asks, "Want to dance?" So much for that one.

I stand there, hoping to look like I am enjoying the music. I love to dance and hate to watch from the sidelines. Everyone is paired off here. Better walk around. I feel slightly ridiculous walking slowly through the crowd. I see my new friend, talking to a man. Good for her! She knows how to work a room! I know, too—in my head, anyway!

I see an opening, a good-looking man. Small talk. He's not as smart as he looks. And he's not very interested. Neither am I. Wander again. There's my friend, talking to another man. She hails me and introduces me to him. We talk. It is difficult to make ourselves heard over the music and chatter. She leaves to continue her rounds. The man is interesting, and we have some things in common. Whew! This is what I came for. I enjoy getting to know this nice person. My feeling about the room shifts from sensing it as an uncomfortable series of obstacles to feeling it as a more inviting place. I think I'll get his phone number rather than just giving him mine. Then I can call him if I want to, rather than waiting for him to call me.

As I drive home I have mixed feelings. There must be a better way! If the perfect man for me had been there, I would have had no way of knowing it. I feel embarrassed that the situation reduced me to this level of social insecurity. The man I met might be interesting, but my reaction might have been simply the relief of meeting *someone*. I tell myself, "You must go out and meet people," but I also hope this is the very last time I put myself through that kind of experience! What other options are there?

Informal Meetings in Your Regular Activities

Of course, you can meet people through activities or situations in which you are already involved, such as work, church, or professional organizations. Friends (or friends of friends) may be a rich source of possibilities if you let them know you are interested. Going out with people you encounter in the course of your daily life is good, since you have already seen them in a more familiar setting. However, this may not be best for you. Do not put up with someone who is not good for you because of his or her easy proximity.

In spite of the limitations, one advantage to activities designed specifically for singles is that you and everyone else involved is making a statement of readiness to meet new potential partners. For example, Betty was bemoaning her difficulty in meeting men appropriate for her. I was surprised because she was young, attractive, and outgoing. I asked what she had done to meet men. She said, "There are men at work. Of course, most of them are married. I go to parties and weddings when I'm invited, but most of the men are with someone. I don't do singles things. That seems so desperate."

"Desperate" expresses the feeling among many that it is more romantic to meet someone "accidentally" and that it's not quite okay to even admit that you want to meet potential partners. But since choosing a mate is one of the most important and complex decisions you make in your life, it deserves your full attention. Giving yourself the opportunity to meet a number of potential partners is a part of this process.

My husband, Fred, and I met at a professional conference. Our situation was not an easy one, as we lived in different cities, several hours apart. We had to condense the getting-acquainted process into small bits of time, especially at first. We were both aware that short, intense visits could produce an unrealistic romantic aura.

I had polished my Ideal Partner list sufficiently to know he was worth the effort and patience I needed to put forth. I was aware enough of my own patterns to know what to watch for, and I was willing to take all the time necessary to be sure we were right for each other. I eventually moved from southern California to the city in northern California where he lived (an area where I had previously lived and to which I wanted to return even before we met).

In the two years we spent commuting to be together, we grew closer. We got to know each other's family and friends. But we wanted more time in close proximity before we made a commitment. So when I moved, I rented an apartment five minutes from his and we concentrated on getting to know each other in a more everyday way. We also did some intense couples workshops together, which gave us invaluable tools to deal with the inevitable questions and difficulties that came up. Our decision to be a committed couple came after careful consideration. Not that it wasn't fun. It was magical and special and full of romance! But it was also a sensible way to go about making an extremely important decision.

Your regular activities do offer some opportunities for meeting potential partners. An example of this is the Internet. Computer networks may significantly change "boy meets girl" options in the future. (I recently got to know my first couple who met "online.") However, as the media have documented extensively, it is important to remember that because of the total anonymity of the Internet, people can create and present a completely false image of themselves. Do not get involved with someone without putting appropriate safeguards in place to check the sincerity of the correspondent, and take plenty of time to get to know someone in real-life situations.

If the above methods, requiring little outside your usual routines, are not working for you, other alternatives exist. Among them are:

Computer Dating Services

Computer dating services are proliferating. If you choose this approach, look for one with many members, solid finances, and a staff. Ask what the staff does to help the members, since, in some services, the staff knows the people and can assist you in finding appropriate prospects.

In others, you are totally on your own to look through stacks of large notebooks. Each member is allotted a page in one of the notebooks. For your own entry, you are given questions to answer about your hobbies, job, and family. You can insert your favorite photos of yourself in whatever settings you like. Your own personal videotaped interview can sometimes be made available, which means you are able to view the videos of others as well. Personality questionnaires and values tests may also be options, but be sure to find out whether you are on your own to interpret them. After looking at the notebook pages and videos, when you find an appealing individual, you fill out a request form and turn it in to the service.

Once you decide you would actually like to meet someone, the service lets that other person know and his or her response is passed on to you. The phone number of each of you is supplied to the other. An advantage to this system is that women are as free to choose as men. And there is no face-to-face embarrassment or pressure to say "yes." There is a fee, of course—anywhere from $500 for six months to $1800 for life (a singles group for life?).

These memberships are probably not worth the price if you join, then just sit and wait for the phone to ring. You must really be willing to use the facilities to get your money's worth. If you do not fit the stereotypes, you may risk many rejections, even if they are not face-to-face. Typically, men are looking for younger, beautiful women and women are looking for successful, good-looking men. (If you do not fit into these categories, you might not want to invest in this kind of service. Instead, find places to meet people where you can more adequately show your own uniqueness.) If you do connect with someone, meeting in a public place is almost always a good idea, to minimize your exposure in case you find the person objectionable.

The process of thinking through how to present yourself and determining your expectations is one value of joining these services, but don't forget that you can do the same thing without joining a group and paying their price.

Special-Interest Dating Groups

You may find simpler versions of singles organizations oriented toward people with special interests, like Advanced Degrees and Sierra Singles, as well as church groups. Sports-oriented groups, such as those involving skiing, tennis, hiking, and mountain climbing can be excellent ways to meet people who like to do the same things you do. Music or art groups may plan outings for singles, too. One of the most widespread and successful singles groups is Parents without Partners. For singles with children, this group provides activities that include children, as well as adult activities. Parties, picnics, outings, and speakers on parenting skills or other interests of the group are offered. Expenses are kept low. Parents without Partners is commonly listed in the telephone book.

Some groups supply lists of short "ads." You choose people you'd like to know more about and request the "long form," which gives additional information, including address and/or telephone number. Then you can contact the person and meet, if the idea is mutually agreeable. Other groups have evening events to attend or athletic teams or tournaments or trips, where you can meet people who have at least this one interest in common. These groups are much less expensive than the computer services because they do not generally maintain an office. To learn about such groups, you may need to talk to other singles, or they may advertise in newspapers and small "throw-away" papers, or in athletic clubs.

Dinner Parties

There are also groups that host dinner parties for singles. The individual makes a reservation, pays a fee, and attends the function. Attendees are asked to exchange chairs between courses so they can meet various others more easily, a format that provides a safe atmosphere in which to talk with a number of new people. These groups are advertised in singles papers or by word of mouth, though you may need to talk to other singles to find out about them, as many rely heavily on personal references.

Personal Ads

Another possibility is personal ads in magazines or newspapers. With reputable publications this is safe, since the replies are sent to the magazine or newspaper, which forwards them to you. As with the other methods, you can meet the person in a public place for lunch or just talk on the phone. You are likely to encounter fewer rejections using this process, because only those who are interested will answer your ad. You will want to be very discriminating in screening the "applicants" for your attention, but at least you will find people to screen (if you write a good ad). I have known happy couples who met this way.

Structured Group Meetings

An excellent method for getting acquainted with new people is a highly structured group meeting for singles, in which those attending actually get to know something about others who come. One such group, based on the East Coast, is called "The Meeting Place." (I attended one of these evening meetings in Los Angeles that was sponsored by The Learning Annex.) Activities are planned so participants have the opportunity for a short conversation with almost everyone in the room before the evening is over. Participants are divided into frequently changing groups of four to six people. Lists of questions are provided, to be answered by each person. The questions are designed so people feel free to say something genuine about themselves.

In one such group I found, before the evening was over, that I had come to know a little about many people, and they were an amazingly interesting, varied crowd. How different from the unstructured singles meetings where I have met only a few people and often the loud music prevented quality conversation of any kind. I feel this type of event, an intelligent way to meet new people, has the potential to enjoy widespread popularity.

Creating Your Own Group

If you are enterprising, you could get your single friends and acquaintances together and plan your own events. I know of women who have done this by organizing potluck dinners for friends and the friends of friends. Each woman guest brought some food and a single male friend to introduce to others at the dinner.

Introduction Services

These services offer more personal attention to your needs and often appeal to busy people. Some cater to those with special interests, such as classical music. One such service, *Together*, originating in Ashland,

Massachusetts, and with agencies in other states, relies on "counselors" who are chosen because they are intuitive and are sensitive to individuals' needs. I was impressed by the fact that, before clients actually meet, they are not permitted to see pictures of each other. This service stresses common interests, values, and temperaments as determined by tests and interviews. They offer five specially selected introductions for a given price.

These kinds of agencies are more expensive than some others because of the individual attention they give. Numbers of members and their successful matchings, as well as financial viability, would be important to investigate before signing up. If you can afford it and are too busy or too shy to meet people in other ways, or if you have specific needs, this might be a good investment. It is, however, only for those serious about finding a lasting relationship.

As we have seen, choosing to be in a committed relationship is a life-changing decision, and knowing how to meet a partner and being available are both important. Equally important, however, is knowing the different kinds of relationships you can get into. That is the subject of the next chapter.

9

ADDICTION OR COMMITMENT?
How to Tell the Difference

Imagine observing couples at a gathering. Among them you see people who are: apparently unable to keep from touching each other; comfortable moving to opposite sides of the room, only occasionally looking at each other; busily flirting with different people; separate from the crowd, talking seriously to each other.

Which partners are giving evidence of a comfortable, secure relationship and which are feeling unfulfilled or insecure? Which partners are comfortably committed to each other and which are hanging onto addictive relationships? Can you tell from superficial observation? If you were to ask them, would they know the difference between addiction and commitment? Probably not.

This chapter will give you some clues about how to answer those questions for yourself in regard to your own present or future relationship. First of all, though, you may ask, "Why commitment?" That word often has fearful associations, especially when you look at divorce statistics or remember your painful experiences with your own or your parents' love relationships.

Why Commitment?

Commitment is no longer synonymous with marriage. Many couples today are choosing to be in committed relationships without marriage.

The decision about marriage is complicated by romantic history, family values, financial considerations, age, and religious beliefs. These days it is an individual decision, not necessarily to be taken for granted, as it was in the 1950s and earlier. For example, Fred and I spent a long time thinking about marriage, considering legal and financial aspects as well as our personal feelings. In the end, our family values were an important influence. One day, for instance, my four-year-old grandson asked across the dinner table, "Why are you not married? You chose each other." Neither Fred nor I had an answer appropriate for him. All the couples he knew were married.

But for us, commitment to the relationship came before consideration of marriage. By "commitment" I mean a thoughtful, intentional decision to give the long-term value of the relationship itself a greater priority than the short-term and often conflicting needs of the individuals, whether they are married or not. This intent provides a framework for relationship. With the security of knowing one partner is not going to abandon the other, there is the freedom to risk total honesty and vulnerability. With commitment, each knows that when emotional healing is necessary, time exists for it to take place gradually. There is the security for each partner to explore self and other, and to take the big risks of asking directly for what is wanted and needed. There is the security of being able to receive from the other and to learn to give appropriately to the other. Most important, there can be this understanding: "As I give to you, I stretch my own boundaries in ways that truly contribute to my own growth and healing. I chose you for your differences from me as well as for your similarities. Even if the stretching is hard for me at times, I value you for the challenges your needs present to me."

In earlier chapters, I suggested that when you sense an exciting challenge with a new person, you feel what is often called *chemistry*. This is likely to come along with your unconscious wish to finally get some kind of fulfillment you missed as a child. Romantic intimacy can provide the possibility for this emotional completion. Exciting! But this same quality can also cause problems for you again—now, as an adult—in the same way it did when you were a kid. Dangerous!

Commitment includes an option for making the necessary correction. Addiction, however, involves continuing the same old hurtful pattern you experienced earlier in your life. An example:

Andy and Ruth

Andy and Ruth, a married couple in their twenties, came to me for help in understanding why they were having the same arguments over and over. We began by exploring how their marriage was similar to their parents' marriages.

Ruth's perception of her parents' marriage, which ended in divorce, was that her mother constantly gave up her own needs to try to please her father. Ruth therefore made an important decision: in her marriage, she would be strong, never weak like her mother was.

Andy saw his parents' marriage as one in which his mother held the power and his father was conciliatory and accommodating. Andy learned that he could achieve a feeling of harmony by doing what his father did and surrendering to his mother's control.

In their counseling work with me, Andy and Ruth learned to recognize that when they married, their pasts fit together like pieces of a puzzle. Ruth, having decided never to be weak, chose someone accommodating, who would not contradict her. Andy, who had learned to be accommodating, chose someone powerful who would take charge and be strong.

They had a perfect fit. The only problem was that once the honeymoon period was over, Ruth discovered that Andy's "giving in" tendencies, which seemed so pleasant to her, disguised his real feelings of being powerless. He tended to withdraw protectively and she felt she couldn't get close to him. Andy realized that Ruth's controlling tendencies were not so much a product of genuine strength as they were a compensation for her feelings of insecurity. When they stopped living on the surface of their relationship and their feelings of powerlessness and insecurity began to emerge, they were faced with a choice: break up, divorce, and find new partners (with whom they would have the same old problems) or take this opportunity to use their struggles as a way to learn and grow. Since they were *committed*, determined to make their marriage work, they chose to learn from their differences.

Andy's warmth and ability to be conciliatory softened Ruth's hard edges. Ruth's outspoken manner taught Andy to be more honest about his feelings. His growing openness also made him more aware of his feelings. He became more autonomous and self-confident, realizing he needed to stand up for himself, even if it produced an argument. He needed to learn from Ruth's directness rather than being intimidated by it. Ruth recognized that she needed to temper her directness and respect Andy's opinions, not try to control him as his mother had.

Suppose they had not been committed to making their marriage work. Ruth would have felt more and more resentful of Andy's "weakness." Andy would have pulled farther and farther away from her abrasiveness. Very soon the initial attraction of his soft and loving ways and her strength and openness would have degenerated into her dominance and his withdrawal. The marriage would have been a disaster.

So the difference between a productive, mutually fulfilling, maturing relationship and that potential disaster was one important thing: *commitment* — which included a determination to learn from differences rather than continuing to give in to hurtful patterns. Without commitment, they'd have been alone again, out looking for new partners, carrying the same immature patterns along with them. With commitment, they stimulated growth and maturity in each other.

One important factor in making a commitment work is to recognize the reason for the attraction, which is often the "fit" of opposite behaviors, then to consciously and affirmatively work with those differences rather than allowing them to provoke arguments. A couple's ability to do this depends on the willingness of the partners to explore their habitual patterns. Learning of the hurts and fears behind their behavior empowers them to help each other heal and grow. A commitment to the relationship is necessary if sufficient time and attention are to be available for such changes to happen.

Andy and Ruth also could have stayed together and painfully continued the patterns that were established by their childhood experiences, each secretly hoping the other would change. Or they could have decided that any expectation of marriage beyond what they learned as children was unrealistic or unsafe. They would then have been stuck in an *addictive* relationship.

Andy might have said to himself, "Women are demanding. You just have to keep your distance from them. That's the way marriage is." And Ruth might have said something like, "I'm used to taking charge and I like it that way. We're not close, but what else can you expect of a man?" Andy and Ruth, had they created an addictive relationship, would not have been able to get their real needs met and nothing would have changed, unless one or the other of them began getting those needs met by someone else or decided that continuing in the marriage was too painful.

What Is an Addictive Relationship?

What, then, is an addictive relationship? It is one in which there is an unconscious wish to fulfill old needs and each partner keeps longing for those needs to be fulfilled but *is not* making growth changes in himself or herself.

For example, Tom and Sue are typical of couples I counsel. Tom is a "distancer," or passive, and Sue a "clinger," or needy. (Of course, the roles might also have been reversed, with his being the "clinger" and her being the "distancer.")

Here is Sue talking about Tom:

He and I saw each other almost daily for a year. We told each other about everything that was happening in our lives. He was in advertising and I spent time on weekends helping him with his latest presentation. He helped me by fixing things in my house. That was the good side. On the other side, I could never count on him. He would be warm and supportive one day and the next day he would treat me as though I were the last priority in his life. On those bad days, he put me down. He wouldn't touch me. Then I felt awful and tried hard to please him. When that didn't work, I finally went away to lick my wounds.

Later, in his own time and in his own way, he would become warm again. Then I would feel complete, like a half that had become whole. The good times were so wonderful that I forgot the pain.

Naturally, I always wanted to be more intimate. It felt so good to me and it seemed, at those moments, to feel good to him, too. As our relationship went on, as I wanted more time together and more intimacy, the uncomfortable moments became more frequent. The more I tried to please him, the more he became verbally abusive and less dependable.

This is an addictive kind of relationship. Tom is experiencing a familiar scenario—a woman "crowding" him. What he did as a child was to withdraw, and he also does that with Sue. Sue is in an old, familiar, painful scenario, too. When she asks for something from Tom, she doesn't expect to get it, but she tries harder until she finally gives up and backs off. Only then does Tom come toward her. Not much fun for either of them. But because these ways of behaving bring up old, intense feelings, the relationship feels very exciting when it is good and that keeps them going. Or it did until Sue had enough. This is what happened:

I blew up one day—told him I'd had it! We'd been through this cycle so many times. This time was it! I told him I was through.

Later, I talked to my friend Betty about the situation. She said, "It sounds like you're addicted. And do you know how to break an addiction? You don't taper off. 'Just one more' won't do it. You have to quit cold turkey!"

I thought about it and realized she was right. I could go on with this roller coaster for the rest of my life, even though it took so much of my attention that I wasn't getting on with my career. I didn't meet other people socially. I neglected my women friends. Tom certainly didn't want the commitment of marriage.

I told myself that if I was tempted to call Tom, I would call Betty first.

The first week my body ached. I had no energy. I thought about Tom most of the time. Memories of the bad times seemed to fade out. I tried not to think about the warm, loving times. I stayed busy. In the middle of the night it was hard to sleep.

After a week he called me. It was good to talk, but I kept my determination and did not bite when he hinted about our getting together. He would never come right out and say "I want to see you," even though I knew he missed me.

The following weekend I was busy with a class during the days, but on Saturday night and Sunday night I was alone. Sunday night I came home from class at dusk. It was a lovely evening. I put a lone potato in the oven to bake and went for a walk. In the first two blocks, every step brought back memories. I thought, "I *could* call him. The sunset would be so beautiful from his apartment. We would have dinner and talk, and I would spend the night. Oh, his arms around me would feel so good. There's nobody else in my life like that. I deserve to be loved and held."

But I soon began to hear another voice in the back of my head. I came to a corner, realizing that my feet could take me directly home to that dangerous phone. Instead I pointed my steps around the corner and walked the long way home.

Turning that corner made a difference. The dim voice in the background got louder. "You know it's not going to change. You know you've been waiting and hoping for a long time. Your needs have not been met. In spite of the ache of the last two weeks, you have reconnected with important parts of your life — old friends and your own creativity. At this moment you are in pain, but get through this moment and it will be better. Go home and call Betty."

My step was lighter now. The sunset was lovely. I looked at it and said aloud, "It's my sunset!" I knew I had made it through one more temptation and had taken a step toward once again having control of my life.

Tom, in this example, is typical of a person who is terrified of being engulfed. He wants intimacy yet is afraid of a loss of his identity if he gives in to it. He sees Sue as he did the parents who needed too much from him and could give but little. Because his parents depended on him emotionally, he felt guilty about distancing from them and blamed them for causing his guilt. But he could not openly hurt his parents because, as a child, he needed them too much. He reserved his feelings of resentment for other intimates in his life. So the cycle of intimacy, dependency, and then fear, anger, and distancing perpetually repeated itself in his romantic relationships.

Sue had her own dilemma. She had often been disappointed by her parents. They were too busy and too involved in their own problems to provide her with consistent attention. Her father didn't give her the feeling of being accepted, and though she was always trying to please him, she seldom felt successful. She kept trying harder to please Tom, too, and her trying never worked. She was addicted to the times he seemed to accept and cherish her — which was what she had wanted so much from her father.

Both Tom and Sue looked to each other to get the kind of love neither got from their parents. They did not consciously recognize their childhood pain and they *used* each other to express the resentments they could not express earlier in their lives. For both, the emphasis was on getting needs met by the partner and in protecting themselves from vulnerability.

With them, as with couples in other addictive relationships, despair and ecstasy prevailed; their situation was tumultuous rather than secure. It was a drain on their energies, characterized by habitual, repetitive, destructive behavior rather than long-range change for the better.

Sue and Tom and many others like them might have stayed together in one way or another for a long time. But theirs was not a committed relationship in the healthy sense. Each was unconsciously attempting to resolve old personal issues by *using* the other and neither was truly available to the other.

The issues of an addictive couple can be resolved in several ways. The partners can stop seeing each other, thus breaking the addictive pattern. But such a choice would not resolve the unconscious issues and there would be no healing. Someone in Sue's position (the "clinger" in a couple, male or female) is more apt to seek help and resolve her issues, because she is more aware of the pain. However, if she seeks to avoid the pain by feeling only anger and blaming Tom, thus avoiding any sense of responsibility in the matter, she will probably not seek help. She will be likely to repeat this pattern with another partner.

The pain felt by Tom (the "distancer") is less conscious. He may assume an attitude that declares "women are too demanding" and be inclined to have increasingly shallow relationships. Or he may seek help if his pain from loss is great enough or if his self-awareness develops.

Having stopped seeing each other, these two people could go on and on, drifting from one addictive relationship to another, until one or both of them became thoroughly disenchanted by romance. Another solution might be better, however. The couple could separate, each heal on his or her own, then find other partners with whom to form new, healthier relationships.

Yet another solution, provided the partners are compatible with each other in significant areas of their lives, would be to make a solid commitment to the relationship and use the relationship itself to heal. The rewards could be substantial but the process might be difficult work for both.

In order for this solution to succeed, communication between the partners must become open and honest, with increasing awareness of feelings. For most people in this dilemma, an outside "coach" or therapist is highly desirable or even necessary. Without skilled professional help, such a relationship can easily spiral downward, as the "clinger" tries harder to make things work and the "distancer" runs away faster.

The repetitive interaction in an addictive relationship may be acted out with jealousy, money, power, or other issues, but at its core the conflict is rooted in unmet needs of childhood. These needs felt like necessities for survival back then, which leads to the intense attraction to someone to whom you now give the power to fulfill or *fail to fulfill* them.

Doing things for another to promote one's own survival (or the survival of the relationship, which may *feel* like personal survival) is not a gift of loving action, freely given. Instead, it is done from the fear of loss. This difference may be subtle, yet it is crucially important (more about that later).

Think about past relationships in your life. Are you likely to gravitate to addiction? From the Relationship History or the Remembering Childhood exercises, you can almost certainly get some hints about the initial reasons you were attracted to certain people in the past and the reasons you subsequently broke up, and you can use this information to discover your tendencies with regard to possible addictions in the present.

What Is a Committed Relationship?

We have looked at addiction in relationships. Now let's explore commitment. First let's examine the changes in the meaning of commitment that have occurred since the 1950s. At that time, marriage and commitment were synonymous. The "normal" thing was getting married, working hard to be successful, and having children (then grandchildren). Of course! Then the 1960s brought the sexual revolution and a whole new set of attitudes about relationships. The feminist movement was strong. Betty Friedan's book, *The Feminine Mystique*, gave voice to the anger women were feeling about their traditional roles. Men as well as women began to see the importance of questioning whether their needs in relationship were being met.

Fritz Perls, a Gestalt therapist and author, wrote a statement of this position that was reprinted on posters and widely quoted and accepted as a desirable viewpoint. In his 1969 book *In and Out of the Garbage Pail*, he wrote:

> *I do my thing and you do your thing.*
> *I am not in this world to live up to your expectations*
> *And you are not in this world to live up to mine.*
> *You are you and I am I,*
> *And if by chance we find each other, it's beautiful.*
> *If not, it can't be helped.*

Perls's statement and the point of view it expressed were the opposite of commitment. It was representative of a common theme at that time and may have been a necessary step in the healthy evolution of relationships, somewhat as adolescence is a necessary step in growing to adulthood. But what followed in the 1970s was an increase in divorces, fifty percent or more in some geographical areas, as people questioned the restrictiveness of the marriage "yoke." They searched for the "real self" and the "perfect partner" who would provide love as well as freedom of expression. Sexual activity outside marriage became the norm for many people. For those of us raised before the 1950s, this was a colossal change. For those who became adults in the 1960s and 1970s, it was confusing. In the 1980s, AIDS entered the picture and put a damper on unrestricted sexual freedom, further confusing the situation.

Many people were influenced in their formative years by the tumultuous changes of the 1960s and 1970s and by the effects those times had on their own lives and families. They are still looking for better ways to relate. Today, in the 1990s, the pre-1960 and post-1960 ideals of relationship are coming together as an expression of longing for both individuality and intimacy. Women are more committed to careers. Men are exploring their inner, intuitive side and are participating to a greater degree in nurturing activities. Both men and women are looking for new ways to create a sense of family security as an anchor in their busy, stressful lives. That is the climate in which we now consider what we mean by commitment.

Ashley Montagu is an excellent source for a definition of love and commitment. An anthropologist, he has observed and weathered many social changes during his long life and has written many books, among which are *Touching* and *The Natural Superiority of Women*. He brings wisdom from his studies about human behavior to the dilemmas of modern society. At a recent lecture, I heard him speak joyfully and respectfully of his wife of many years. His thoughts about love and commitment took this form:

You should marry for friendship, which is another form of love. I will define love in plain English. Love is the ability by demonstrative acts to confer upon the other not only survival benefits, but the awareness that they can depend upon your standing by, ministering to their dependent needs for all those potentialities with which we are born. They can depend upon your giving them all the support and sustenance they require for their growth and development. You encourage of all their inner potentialities. These potentialities are, in human beings, the need for love, the need for friendship, the need for learning, curiosity, wonder, imagination, for fantasizing, for creativity, for explorativeness, for play, music, weeping, touch. These are basic behavioral needs and they are part of our genetic system — they cannot be argued away.

Montagu talks about mutually loving actions satisfying the basic needs of the partners. Fritz Perls, in his 1960s statement, declares that meeting one's own needs is more important than the success of the relationship. This may allow individuals to grow separately, but it does not allow for growth and satisfaction within the relationship. For Perls, love is something you get when another happens to share your path; for Montagu, love is something you create by being a loyal and giving friend.

M. Scott Peck's widely read book *The Road Less Traveled* defines love and commitment this way:

> When we extend ourselves, when we take an extra step or walk an extra mile, we do so in opposition to the inertia of laziness or the resistance of fear . . . . Love is a form of work or a form of courage. Specifically, it is work or courage directed toward the nurture of our own or another's spiritual growth . . . . Since it requires the extension of ourselves, love is always either work or courage. If an act is not one of work or courage, then it is not an act of love. There are no exceptions. The principal form that the work of love takes is attention. When we love another we give him or her our attention; we attend to that person's growth . . . .

and

> Commitment is inherent in any genuinely loving relationship. Anyone who is truly concerned for the spiritual growth of another knows, consciously or instinctively, that he or she can significantly foster that growth only through a relationship of constancy.

Love in a Committed Relationship Means Action

Doing something simply to please your partner or to fill a need of your partner puts love into *action*. "Gift actions," freely given, feel good. They bring the giver deep pleasure and stimulate growth in new and unexpected directions. The receiver may not receive the gift well at first. There may be skepticism ("He'll never do that again!") or the gift may not be offered exactly the way the receiver wanted it. Nevertheless, loving acts foster the feeling of love in both giver and receiver.

Ideally, loving acts are opportunities to do things that are a "growth stretch" for the giver. For example:

Tanya is fast-moving and impatient. She is married to stable, patient, slow-to-change Ramon. (His stability is what first attracted her.) When Tanya wants something to change, instead of expecting it to happen immediately, she prepares Ramon for the change, sharing ideas about the process and asking his opinions. She waits while he gets used to these new ideas. She has discovered that by giving her husband this "gift," she also sometimes avoids mistakes herself by making more careful decisions.

Ramon, as his "gift" to his wife, carefully considers her requests and genuinely looks for ways to adjust to change rather than reacting with his habitual resistance. He has found that the changes Tanya initiates often benefit both of them. Each has given something to the other; each has received satisfaction and experienced growth.

Other kinds of "gift actions" are to be found in the ordinary process of daily life. For example, a man not used to cooking could surprise his partner by cooking for her when she is not feeling well or is busy. Many little gifts can be offered, such as noticing and commenting on things one appreciates about the other or being gentle and supportive when the other is under pressure. These are small things, but the more they happen in a relationship, the more two people can learn from each other and grow in their enjoyment of their relationship. This kind of giving needs to be reciprocal. If it becomes one-sided, it can build resentment in the giver and guilt in the receiver.

AN EXAMPLE OF COMMITMENT

The needs and challenges of a young family are a test of commitment. Let's look now at a couple who have lived through that test and enriched their lives through their commitment to each other.

Joe and Dorothy, who have been married more than thirty years, still enjoy being together and doing interesting things as a couple. They are wonderfully affectionate with each other, though sometimes they appear to quibble about small things. When I paid closer attention, however, I noticed that their quibbling was purposeful. Through it, they both expressed wants and needs, came to consensus, and moved to action. I decided to interview them about their commitment to their marriage.

I learned that some aspects of their courtship and wedding set the stage for their commitment. When they met, they were attending colleges some distance apart but lost no time getting to know each other. (On their first date, they discovered similarities in background, including the fact that their fathers, both pharmacists, had actually met each other.) The young couple soon became more deeply acquainted. On their sixth date, Joe — following the custom of the day — asked Dorothy to wear his fraternity pin. But before she said "yes," she spent an hour quizzing him on issues important to her. "Do you want children? If we couldn't have any, would you be open to adoption?" She was already excited by Joe, but took commitment very seriously, wanting to make sure she knew what she was committing to.

Joe was not put off by her questions. In fact, he was intrigued and even more interested in her. From that time, they wrote to each other daily and focused on creating a relationship both could enthusiastically commit to. Engagement and wedding plans followed rapidly.

A story Dorothy told about their wedding night gave me an idea about their commitment to making their plans work out.

"We were so anxious to be together that we arranged for me to complete my degree in three years instead of four. The date of the wedding had to be arranged around the seasonal demands of our fathers' businesses, which meant I had to take an eight-hour exam for a teacher's credential the day after the wedding.

"My mother gave me a gorgeous white satin nightgown, and on our wedding night I put it on and came out in it. Joe took a look at me, grinned, and said, 'Okay, sit down and I'll quiz you for an hour for your exam.' I passed the exam the next day.

"We were both focused on our goals and we knew we had the rest of our lives together. That kind of pragmatism and mutual support is an important part of our commitment to each other and to our marriage."

Three children later, Joe was traveling on business half the time. Dorothy was caring for home and kids. Both were stressed and lonely, needing ways to maintain their excitement and closeness. One method they worked out was a commitment by Joe to phone home every twenty-four hours, even if he was overseas. To deal with Dorothy's boredom with her role at home, they found weekend couples workshops, which stimulated them and stretched them to grow. They were also in an encounter group for a time.

These experiences added to the things they could discuss and provided some of the fun that made life exciting. They came through a difficult time with their closeness not only intact, but also stronger. They were good parents and close to their children, but they remained strong in their commitment to themselves as a couple and found ways to share their interests with their children.

I asked if they ever questioned their marriage commitment. Dorothy laughed and said, "Oh, we fought! I spent some nights in a motel when I was mad at Joe. He could be pretty dominating." And Joe added, "I learned to back off. I used to blame her a lot. I used to be sarcastic when I could have just been listening. Then I learned better ways in a 'fighting fair' workshop we went to. My parents fought a lot and weren't very good role models." Dorothy said, "My parents played lots of manipulative games with each other, so it was important to me not to do that, but rather to express myself clearly. Joe liked that."

Today, after more than three decades of marriage, Joe says, "I consider every day a holiday and every meal a banquet. We work so we can play. Both of us now have offices at home. We plan our lives so we do interesting things. We usher at performances, attend lectures, and belong to interesting groups so we interact with a wide variety of fascinating people. Once a month we go to museums. Once a week we square dance. We enjoy being together, and part of that is stretching ourselves to find new things to learn about and experience."

I saw that they both say "yes" to life and living. There is great zest and excitement in their approach to life together. And given their commitment to the quality as well as to the longevity of their relationship, they plan to continue living that way into a very old age.

Addiction and Commitment: The Differences

Learning to recognize the differences between an addictive and a committed relationship is important in deciding whether a particular romance will bring satisfaction. There are couples who are so far apart and whose differences are so toxic that they cannot, even with great effort, bring satisfaction to each other, despite their once having "fallen in love." One client, who gave up an addictive romance then created a healthy, loving relationship after a period of growth, put it this way:

> In the addictive romance, I felt "hungry" for him. On those occasions when he was good to me in the ways that were important to me, I was high with exhilaration. It was like having a gourmet meal when you're really hungry. But those highs inevitably led to lows, and I was hungry again. I would try anything to be fed. I was always questioning our commitment—his and my own—though our time together was intense and exciting and hard to give up!
>
> At first, in this new, more healthy relationship, I was sometimes afraid I would feel hungry, but he comes through for me. I am satisfied. Gradually I came to trust him and I can be more fully myself than I ever have been. We have disagreements but we know we will work them out. The intensity of highs and lows is not there. The excitement produced by that tumult is replaced by a glow of certainty in our love for each other. We are committed to growing together, and it feels wonderful.

Recognizing different kinds of relationships is an important part of choosing a romantic partner. To have both excitement and serenity is possible, though this may require some special learning on your part—and you may need help. The next chapter will offer suggestions about how to find the most appropriate assistance —as an individual or as a couple— should you decide to seek such help.

10

HELP FOR LOVE'S HURTS

Do you continually choose partners who, in one way or another, present you with the same problems you first encountered at home as a youngster? Often, as surprising as it seems, many of us do exactly that. Such romantic choices are, of course, made with little awareness of what we're actually doing. And though we may want to "get it right this time" as adults, we are likely to set ourselves up, unconsciously, to fail. If your own unproductive patterns from the past are still affecting you to a significant degree, you may take on a relationship that has overwhelming challenges. And with your having done that, the time may arrive when you can use some good, competent outside help.

How do you know whether you need outside help? If your relationship history shows a pattern of more unhappiness than happiness or you find you are hurting yourself and/or others or you have simply run out of useful ideas about how to proceed, you may need a helper, or helpers, along this path.

A therapist? You may think, "I'm not in *that* much trouble! I can figure this out myself." Indeed, you may be able to, but it's your happiness that's at stake and you may be going around and around like a squirrel in a cage without realizing it. You may need an objective outsider to help you out of that cage.

What do I mean by "therapist"? (If you're bothered by the word "therapist," substitute "counselor" or "consultant.") What is therapy all about? In the 1950s and before, therapy was seen by most people as lying on a couch weekly (or even more often) for years. It was expensive and only for very rich or very disturbed people. Since then, however, vast and exciting changes have taken place in the "helping professions" and you may owe it to yourself to know more about current possibilities. For one thing, the stigma of mental illness is no longer attached to therapy. It is now something that smart people do to maximize their potential for fulfillment and growth.

If you are a man or a very independent woman, you may have difficulty admitting the need for help. But if your leg were broken, your needing help would be obvious. For many of us, broken relationships can be just as debilitating as broken limbs and the importance of emotional healing is no less than that of physical healing. In fact, nothing is more central to your happiness than your intimate relationships, and whatever you can do to make that part of your life satisfying will improve the quality of the rest of your life.

The kind of therapy and therapist you choose will vary according to your goals and your situation, so I will only suggest general guidelines for selecting a specific person to work with.

You may have considerations about the cost of therapy. Of course, you should. It is usually expensive. But that should not be a deterrent if your peace of mind is at stake. If expense is a major problem you might want to investigate publicly funded institutions, such as a local Family Service agency or your County Mental Health Department. Some communities have privately funded agencies that deal with special kinds of issues, such as chemical dependency or child abuse. Alcoholics Anonymous and its offshoots — Co-Dependents Anonymous, Adult Children of Alcoholic Parents, Debtors Anonymous, Overeaters Anonymous, and others — are all available without fee. They do not provide therapy as such, but the group support they offer is extremely important and can stabilize a problem or provide an introduction or adjunct to therapy. Colleges and universities that train counselors and therapists are often a good source of interns who work for a minimal fee or none at all, because they are getting supervised experience. Some communities have crisis hotlines, which may be a source of referrals.

In seeking appropriate help for yourself or a loved one, the community phone book or newspaper would be a good place to start, as would a call to the local Chamber of Commerce or City Hall. Certain insurance plans pay some or most of the costs of mental health care, and company health plans often include mental health benefits.

What I will offer here are only general descriptions of the assorted kinds of training and licensing, and the reader should be aware that individual states may differ in their licensing requirements. You might want to find out about the various kinds of licensing your state requires of therapists and also what kinds of training are necessary for the license. These are questions you are clearly entitled to ask any therapist you consider.

Psychiatrists

Psychiatrists first become medical doctors, then take additional training to become psychiatrists. They are able to write prescriptions for drugs. Their skills and interests vary greatly, so you would need to ask individuals specific questions about the focus of their work. They are apt to be more expensive than other therapists because of the medical training they must have in addition to their psychiatric training.

Clinical Psychologists

Clinical Psychologists must have a Ph.D. and are trained to do psychological and personality testing as well as therapy. Their approaches to therapy vary widely, depending on their training and interests.

Marriage and Family Counselors

Therapists who are licensed Marriage, Family, and Child Counselors (in California and some other states) or who belong to the American Association of Marriage and Family Therapists (a nationwide organization) emphasize relationship therapy in their training and experience. They must have a master's degree and specified experience to qualify.

Social Workers

In some states, licensed Clinical Social Workers are more common and do a variety of types of counseling with individuals and families. They must have at least a master's degree and specified experience as well. Many states require license candidates to pass an examination in addition to completing academic training and supervised experience.

Any of the above licensed therapists may use a variety of the forms and techniques described below. To find out the focus of any one therapist's work, there is no substitute for asking questions.

A MENU OF POSSIBLE GROWTH THERAPIES

An exciting variety of therapies is available for you to choose from. Many of these are relatively new, having been developed or refined in the past 20-30 years.

Individual (One-to-One) Verbal Therapy

This is probably the most common form of therapy, but within its broad range are many specialties. To make an informed choice, you should ask the therapists you consider to describe what they specialize in and what their training was. Most experienced therapists also have specific training beyond their basic degrees and licensing. Ask about that, as well as their interests and background.

Therapists work from various fundamental perspectives. The Freudian focuses most on the inner conflicts of an individual person. The Family Systems orientation concentrates on interactions within families and how each individual is affected by and affects this system. Jungian therapists have specialized training beyond basic psychology and their focus is on the teachings of Carl Jung. Dream analysis and working with archetypes are included in this perspective. Another category is Humanistic Psychology, which offers a holistic approach to the entire person: mind, body, and spirit. Transpersonal Psychology has a similar orientation, with an emphasis on realms of consciousness that transcend the personal.

Some of the interesting methodologies therapists use include Gestalt, Voice Dialogue, Transactional Analysis, Rational Emotive Therapy, Narrative Therapy, Self Psychology, Control Mastery, and Object Relations, along with many, many others. These may sound strange if you are not familiar with them, but they are just simple tools, or methods, devised to help you speed up the process of understanding and insight that is a first step in behavioral change. Asking prospective therapists to explain the methods they use is entirely appropriate.

Behavior Modification and Brief Therapy are methods that work with changing behavior first and assuming that attitudinal changes will follow. The success of these kinds of therapies is dependent on the client's being motivated to follow the suggestions of the therapist between sessions.

Couple Therapy

This consists of one or two therapists working with a couple. For several important reasons, this is the kind of therapy I recommend for people in a significant relationship. A primary reason is that having just one other person outside the relationship to whom you tell your intimate thoughts (as in individual therapy) may create a "triangle," with your partner on the outside. The result is thus contrary to your purpose, which is to become closer to your partner. Also, for one person to grow while the other person does not grow is dangerous for the partnership.

The statistics on relationship longevity when one partner does individual therapy and the other does not, show quite convincingly that couple therapy is more effective in helping to promote happy relationships. Certainly circumstances exist in which couple therapy would not be best; however, "I'm fine but my partner is sick [or wrong]" probably would not qualify. Troublesome issues in intimate partnerships involve both people, and exciting benefits are available when both partners are in the room and witness each other's work.

This kind of therapy may sometimes focus on relationship issues directly and sometimes on individual issues that affect the relationship.

Any of the methods described under Individual Therapy may be used, in addition to other, more specialized methods, such as asking couples to exchange chairs and identities during the session, so they can more readily get into each other's feelings. Many such techniques are available that couple therapists can use to help couples sort out their issues.

Divorce Therapy

Divorce therapy is extremely useful in completing the grief process and bringing about an emotional divorce. This is particularly crucial if children are involved. I offered this kind of therapy for a number of years and came to believe that a male/female therapist team is usually most effective. Each partner in the dissolving relationship needs to feel supported and understood by someone of the same sex. (Of course, a team is likely to be more expensive, so if cost is a major consideration, don't be reluctant to work with just one therapist.) This approach can circumvent much legal expense and actually save money that might have been spent on destructive legal battles. Such battles often leave people scarred and bitter, whereas therapy is a healing process.

Premarital Therapy

This may be the most useful support a couple can have. Identifying basic issues (the ones that cause initial attraction as well as those that contain potential challenges) before problems become entrenched makes practical sense. Armed with conscious awareness of these issues, a couple can work together to heal and grow rather than create unproductive conflict.

Sex Therapy

Sex therapy is still another kind of couple (but sometimes individual) work. Sexual problems are relatively simple to treat, though often they are embedded in more complex relationship issues. You are cheating yourself if you keep putting up unnecessarily with strictly sexual problems.

Many licensed therapists have some training in human sexuality and sex therapy. Those who have extended their training may specialize in this field. You might want to inquire about the person's sex therapy training during your interview.

The reputable therapist *never* makes sexual overtures to a client. "Homework assignments" may be given, to be carried out in the privacy of the client's home with his or her own intimate partner.

Family Therapy

This can be an extremely effective, life-changing experience. It requires that a significant number of the members of a family agree to meet with the therapist or cotherapists. For this work, the therapist should have a background in family systems. He/she would work with various members of the family to sort out the ways in which their interactions are not bringing them satisfaction and to help them learn new ways of relating.

On one occasion, I participated (as a client) in a four-hour session with my mother, brother, and sister. My father was deceased, but we had his photograph there to help us interact with him as well. This one experience changed certain ways our family related and did a great deal to heal old wounds for me. It has been the single most powerful event among the variety of processes I have undertaken to help me have a healthy, happy romantic relationship.

Group Therapy

This is an effective and less expensive way to grow. A small group of people meet regularly with one therapist or two cotherapists. A relationship-oriented group may be all single people, all couples, or a mixture of singles and couples. The advantage of a group is that members learn from their interactions with one another. This is particularly valuable for finding out the impact you have on others and can be very helpful if you are, in general, having trouble connecting with members of the opposite sex. For this purpose you would obviously benefit most from a group that includes men and women.

But same-sex groups can also be valuable as supportive, safe places. From personal experience I have found that men especially gain from men's groups, because of the difficulty they have in our culture in talking with one another about personal issues, and particularly personal male issues.

Couples can learn a great deal from each other, and couples groups can be effective places for getting feedback from others about your interactions with your partner. Often the "blind spots" you have about yourselves can be readily seen by others, who then mirror their perceptions back to you, enabling you to see things in ways you otherwise could not. If you are in a relationship that is not working as well as you would like it to, this kind of therapy can help you clarify whether you want to stay in the relationship and work to improve it.

One advantage of groups is that methods can be used that cannot be used otherwise. Sometimes, for example, the therapist will have group participants pretend to be members of a family, or bosses, or other important characters not in the room who are important targets for someone's feelings. This may be done in the form of psychodrama, with the whole group participating, or in a simple format involving just two or three individuals.

Body Therapies

This group of therapies is based on the theory that certain emotions are locked into the muscles of our body and remain that way unless we do something to unlock them. We tend to develop muscle "armor" that restricts our freedom of expression. Thus, a childhood trauma, for instance, could become part of our musculature, affecting how we react to circum-stances. Sometimes a combination of verbal and body therapies is particularly effective if you want/need to push through a difficult transition area or a stuck place.

These techniques include, among others, Reichian therapy, bioener-getics, biofeedback, Rolfing, Feldenkrais, and the Alexander Technique. Licensing and training for body therapies is not uniform, so you will need to ask questions. Some licensed therapists (including some psychiatrists) use body therapy as a specialty — notably Reichian and bioenergetic techniques. Body massage of various kinds, while not psychological therapy, can be a helpful stress-reducer, especially if it is used while you are going through a difficult time.

Other Therapies

Hypnosis is one skill that may be practiced by a person trained in this specialty but not trained in psychology. (However, hypnosis can be and often is also a valuable tool when used by a licensed therapist.)

Though spiritual counselors, or counselors in a church or synagogue, may or may not be trained as therapists, they can often provide assistance that is, at least in part, based on spiritual/religious beliefs they share with a client.

Other therapies that may be used by licensed therapists or by people who are trained only in a particular technique include such processes as rebirthing and past-life (or regression) therapy.

HIRING A THERAPIST

By now, you may have a general idea about the kind of assistance you are looking for. Finding the right individual therapist or group is next. This is an important decision and one you should consider carefully.

If you've never hired a therapist before, you may have some fear and anxiety about it. This is normal and even healthy. Picking up the phone to make that initial call often feels scary — an experience I've had myself. The anticipation of change can be frightening as well as exciting and freeing.

I encourage people to interview three therapists and choose the one they feel can be most helpful. How you feel with this person, as well as how his/her training and experience fit for you, is important. (All therapists are not equally good, and even a very competent therapist may not feel right to you.) Asking for an introductory interview — perhaps half an hour long — is fair, enabling you to ask questions. Or if an interview is not possible, ask your questions over the phone.

If therapy is to be all it can be for you, choosing carefully is important. Be skeptical of therapists who are too quick to tell you what's wrong, who make assumptions about childhood abuse, or who seem to fit you immediately into a certain category. Do not be afraid to say "no" to a therapist who does not feel right to you. And always remember: you do not have to take care of the therapist. The therapist is there for you, not the other way around. Of course, the usual courtesies — being on time, limiting phone calls, and respecting other appropriate boundaries — are important here, as they are in all professional relationships.

Once you have chosen someone to work with, be as clear as you can about your goals for yourself. A good therapist wants you to do that. What you can do to make your therapy work best, once you have decided to begin the process, is to be open and honest and to follow through on what you and the therapist agree will be helpful for you. Giving you advice is not the therapist's job; the therapist's job is to help you evolve so you can give yourself good advice.

Therapy also goes on between sessions, and there may be "homework assignments" in which you try on new behaviors to see how they feel; in the following session, you discuss what happened. Some therapists will not give assignments at all, and you will simply find yourself beginning to do things differently as your self-understanding shifts.

Therapy can improve the quality of your life, and carefully choosing the person you will work with is important. Remember that therapy will not always be comfortable, but if you are not stimulated to stretch and to grow, you will not be getting your money's worth.

11

HEALTHY RELATIONSHIPS

Healthy relationships are not accidents or matters of luck; they are *creations*. When you have the power that comes from increased awareness of yourself, you can transform negative relationship patterns you picked up from your early family into actual strengths in your adult partnerships.

The negative patterns I learned early in my life brought me to relationships that caused me pain but were also valuable learning experiences, helping me to know what I want and need. Most important, these experiences were powerful incentives for me to grow as a person and to understand the process we all go through in choosing partners. The deep happiness and satisfaction I felt on my wedding day came partly from the recognition that I, with my husband, had finally created the wonderful relationship I had always wanted.

Being part of a couple, at its best, is a learning experience as well as a loving experience. If each person stretches to understand and respond supportively to the vulnerabilities of his or her partner, each can grow. For example, if your worst fear is of abandonment, you can work toward achieving more self-reliance as you allow "space" for your partner's fear of engulfment. Your partner can grow reciprocally, and while learning to experience closeness, fulfill your need for more intimacy.

Take a moment to think about lessons you have learned from problems you encountered in the family you grew up in. How does this knowledge make you vulnerable, both in the sense of being open and in the sense of feeling you need to be defensive to protect yourself? How does it make you stronger? If you find this inquiry difficult, remember that gaining optimum value from the lessons you learned as a child may require determination. But you know you're making progress as you focus more on your own inner feelings rather than other people as the source of your happiness or unhappiness.

More awareness of the parts of yourself that need work will help prepare you for a healthy relationship. This is true whether it's a new relationship or one you desire to strengthen and revitalize.

Can It Really Be Done?

Often people ask me if I know any people who are really happy together. Yes, I do. As a matter of fact, my husband and I are two of them. We took enough time to know each other before we chose to make a commitment, and we enjoy working at our relationship — which we do every day. The others I know who are happy in their relationships enjoy working to keep them exciting. One young wife said, "I don't know what I expected on my wedding day, but the first five years of my marriage have been the best years of my life." I knew, though, that she and her husband were diligent about their marriage "work."

What exactly do they work on? Let's look at some general features of happy, healthy relationships and families.

Features of Partners in Healthy Relationships

1. *They are not bound by pain from the past.* Healthy individuals and families do not habitually re-create old, painful situations in their present lives. As they become aware of and work together to heal those old patterns, they are more free to have comfortable as well as exciting love relationships. Friendship and companionship between them become more meaningful; disagreements are resolved quickly. They have grown together in ways that give them the satisfaction of having "gotten it right

this time," of having transcended old patterns that once triggered defensive or angry reactions. This kind of maturing may begin in early adulthood and continue through a gradual process of increased self-awareness, making defensiveness unnecessary and producing a joyful partnership.

2. *They are flexible.* Sometimes rules are maintained through habit, without current, conscious examination of their appropriateness. Creating new responses as circumstances change is healthy. Rigid rules and unvarying ways of behaving, often developed as protections from fears, are inevitably stifling.

Healthy couples develop the patterns of their relationship with care and thought, rather than blindly following the patterns of their parents or of others. For example, Maria and Lewis found that what worked best for them was to reverse the traditional male/female roles. Maria had a demanding, high-paying job as an executive. She enjoyed her work but needed support at home. Lewis loved to cook and take care of her and their child. The switch required some adjustments in attitudes from them, because it was unconventional, both in terms of current standards and in terms of their childhoods. But they knew it "fit," so they worked out a way to do it, and with good results. I was interested to hear Lewis say to Maria, "I really want some quality conversation with you when you come home," and to hear her answer, "I know you want to talk, but first I need just to be quiet and watch TV." That, of course, was the reverse of the usual gender-specific comments most of us are accustomed to hearing in relationships.

3. *They use and appreciate humor.* Humor, which is closely akin to flexibility, can lighten otherwise difficult times. Being able to stand back and see the ridiculousness of a situation releases pressure.

Humor can also be a double-edged sword. We've all heard someone say something insulting, then follow it with, "Can't you take a joke? I was only kidding." I know one family in which the mother was always the butt of the joke. She laughed, too, but eventually realized her self-esteem was sagging. By that time, she and her husband were divorced, but the children carried on the habit of making fun at Mom's expense. She, however, began to respond differently. Every time they made the "typical" kind of joke, she said, "It's not funny!" Finally her children stopped their put-down humor, realizing it was hurtful to her.

4. *They touch each other appropriately.* Touching is supremely important in intimate relationships. This includes, but certainly is not limited to, a robust, joyful sex life—not according to the criteria of sexy articles advertised on magazine covers, but measured in terms of a pace and style that two partners work out together.

Even the simplest touch can easily communicate more than words, and it obviously does so in a different way than words do. Virginia Satir, an internationally respected family therapist, said we need twelve hugs a day to maintain a healthy emotional connection with others. Without those hugs, we develop what she called a "touch deficit." One man, who wanted his wife to lose weight, was advised by their doctor, "At least five times a day, put both arms around her and apply pressure. You don't have to feel like it. Just do it!" She started losing weight and he learned to enjoy hugging his wife.

5. *They acknowledge each other.* Some self-confident individuals can acknowledge themselves to their own satisfaction, but having a romantic partner who (along with friends) understands and appreciates your accomplishments, large and small, is wondrous balm for the soul.

When I taught nursery school, I had a little boy student who was difficult. He was large and tough. He knew and repeated words that set parents' teeth on edge. He could, and often did, fling his arm out and send another child rolling and crying. Clearly, my constant scolding wasn't helping his behavior to improve.

So I looked hard to find where this boy excelled and I discovered he liked to sing. He knew the words to all the nursery-school songs. It was the key that changed his behavior. Every day I found ways to acknowledge his singing. His attitude changed and he became a happier child—and he was easier to be around. There is, in truth, a "little boy" or "little girl" in each of us, who loves to be appreciated and who, if unacknowledged, may "misbehave."

6. *They establish and respect boundaries.* Where do I begin and where do you end? What is my business and what is yours? When couples

first fall in love, their boundaries tend to melt away dramatically. They are interested in the smallest details of each other's life. After a while, though, that can become suffocating for one or both of them, and they may even quarrel to create distance between themselves.

One husband, Jim, told me of the following incident. He needed to prepare for an important test, but it was still six months in the future. His wife, Margaret, kept mentioning it and urging him to make time to study. One day he said, "I don't want you to bring up my test again! It's my problem and I'll handle it. If I haven't begun to study within six weeks, you're free to say whatever you feel like saying." To his surprise, his wife was relieved that she did not have to take any responsibility or put off anything she wanted to plan because of his test. The "boundary" served them both. To celebrate her feeling of relief, she fixed them both a special candlelight dinner.

Respect for each other's preferences and individuality, or separate identity, is crucial to the health of a relationship.

7. *They communicate.* Communication skills are of great importance in a healthy relationship. (Refer back to chapter 7 for the discussion of learning to communicate feelings honestly and openly and developing the ability and willingness to really listen to others.) Communication works when partners tell the truth about their own feelings and listen not only to the messages but also to the feelings of the other. Don't forget that the way you say something is as important as what you say. Nonverbal messages and tone of voice are powerful communicators. (How many ways can you say, "I love you"? How many "hidden" feelings can you hear behind this simple statement when it is uttered in different ways?)

Perhaps the greatest barrier to authentic communication is a lack of self-awareness. If you don't know what you're feeling, you can't tell your partner about it and your partner can't really know what's going on with you. In the example of Jim and Margaret above, if Jim had not been conscious of his annoyance or had expressed it in terms of blame rather than as an "I" message, his wife would have continued reminding him about the test and he would have continued feeling resentment. Both would have wondered why they felt so dissatisfied and distant — and they'd have missed a great dinner. Neither would have a clue about what the other was feeling. This common kind of lack of communication can not only ruin your day, but also wear away at love.

8. *They handle conflict directly.* Because two people who are alert and constructively assertive are bound to find themselves in conflict now and then, their having effective ways to handle conflict is important. If you feel anger, you need to express it in a way that does not damage the other person. One method is to get the other's permission (and attention) and say what you are feeling (not what is "wrong" with that other person). I have found that doing this takes about 30-60 seconds if it stays focused.

When the frustration is off your chest, you may want to ask for a behavioral change from your partner. It is important that your request be specific and ask for a change in *behavior*, not an attitude change. A negotiation may follow. The negotiation must take both partners' needs into consideration. Sealing this "deal" with a hug is a very good idea.

The most important thing about conflict is to know that it is healthy and that either or both of you can ask for change. Both partners should recognize the importance of being responsive to these requests for change, answering honestly in regard to what they can and cannot actually follow through with.

9. *They learn from each other.* If you are attracted to someone who re-creates a problem you recognize from earlier in your life, learning to handle that "old" problem differently is crucial. (We saw how this works in several examples of couples, beginning with Ted and Emily, the "distancer" and the "clinger.")

If differences between partners are not used for learning, they are bound to become sources of conflict. Two simple examples: Carl, who was goal-oriented, and Frieda, who liked to play and relax, came to appreciate their differences. Carl learned to take time off from pursuing his goals (and enjoy it) and Frieda learned to organize her time better and take pleasure in her accomplishments.

Les and Virginia handled money very differently. Virginia was detailed, concerned about taxes and having the checkbook exactly right. Les liked to earn money but did not like to manage it. Instead of allowing these tendencies to produce conflict, they learned to appreciate each other's contributions. Les valued his wife's skill and cooperated with her efforts, while Virginia recognized that if she wanted it done "right," she had to do it herself. Gradually Les learned about business matters from her, and she learned to relax her concern for every detail. Sometimes it wasn't easy, because each of them had developed attitudes toward money from experiences, some painful, as youngsters. Every time there was a conflict, however, they learned more about each other's hurts. By being willing to stretch and be sensitive, they got closer and became wiser. Instead of allowing their differences to pull them apart, they learned from them.

10. *They have fun together.* The real purpose of being together is to enjoy life with each other more than you would alone. Part of that is enjoying fun together, whether it be a spontaneous dance in the kitchen or an elaborate vacation. Fun is a reward for having created a healthy relationship. For people with busy lives (which is most of us), planning for fun times to balance work and family responsibilities is important. One young couple with little money enjoyed playing simple games together at home. Since he always won when they played cards, they decided to play a kids' game—jacks. At jacks, *she* won, and they giggled at his struggles to manage the little ball in a contest in which his sharp intellect provided him with little advantage.

Another couple, John and Carolyn, had two little children. They enjoyed the smiles of their baby and the pretend situations their little boy led them into. They also loved to take their children to parks and on other excursions. Carolyn said, "It's like being a kid again to see the world through their young eyes." They, obviously, were having fun.

11. *They recognize and understand the stages of life.* For both individuals and couples, development inevitably involves progress through different stages of life. In a healthy relationship, these stages are recognized and the changes they bring are expected and appreciated.

The completion of childhood and the entry into adulthood, for example, is ordinarily followed by a long stage during which energy is focused on family and career. This time—the twenties, thirties, and early forties — is characterized by attention to success and status in the world and to childraising. Balancing the requirements of these two challenging enterprises is not easy. Thus, many couples are now rethinking how they deal with this stage, either postponing having children or finding new ways to combine childraising with work. Many men are sharing responsibility for childcare with their wives instead of being totally absorbed by a career.

The forties commonly stimulate a reevaluation of life goals, which can include questioning the relationship itself. Healthy couples welcome this questioning and are each other's allies in finding out "if that's all there is," perhaps even exploring possibilities for change.

In the fifties and sixties and beyond, with a lessening of family responsibility, individuals tend to look outward, to see what contribution they can make to the lives of others in the community — from the local community to the community of nations. This is often regarded as the time of "eldership." For a couple, looking outward together during this time can be a rich and satisfying experience, with occasions for leisure as well as for personal and spiritual growth — as individuals and as a couple. My husband and I have reached this stage, and life is full and exciting for us.

AN EXAMPLE OF A HEALTHY RELATIONSHIP

All of the foregoing characteristics can usually be found somewhere in a healthy, long-lasting relationship. For example, Susan and Peter exemplify a couple with a healthy relationship. They have been married for twenty-five years, though being with them is like being with people who have recently fallen in love. They are obviously strongly attracted to each other.

What "works" for them? Recently, the three of us went to lunch so I could interview them about their marriage. The conversation was so animated that we forgot about the people around us and I barely tasted my food. The quality of their experience together is obviously the result of much shared understanding and insight. Peter noted, "Neither of us requires much distance from the other. We both think it's wonderful to be loved and to be in love, and we won't do anything to jeopardize that." He was enthusiastic about what attracted him to Susan. "She went out of her way to meet me. She had ideas she was passionate about and she was willing to talk about them. I was impressed—turned on! We have similar values, but different interests. She's athletic. I don't like sports. She likes the arts and is interested in spirituality. I like computers, gardening, politics. We have learned so much from each other because of these different interests." Obviously, they not only accept their differences, but they appreciate them as well.

I asked Susan what she had looked for in a man. Her answer was delivered with passion, eyes sparkling, voice intense. "I wanted a man who would appreciate me for my contribution to the world, not just as a person who could take care of the house. I was determined not to be dependent like my mom.

"Before I met Peter, I dreamed I was a bird trapped in a lovely cage and I wanted out. I was twenty-one and having an identity crisis. My mom sent me to a psychiatrist. He, not living in this more enlightened time, said I would 'ultimately accept the cage.' My reaction was, 'Oh, no I won't! I won't get married!'

"But Peter was different. People always told me I talked too much. I love to talk. And Peter wanted someone who communicated, who was willing to talk about things, so he loved it. Before we got married we lived together, which was not acceptable twenty-five years ago in our Midwestern town. But we were determined not to be trapped in a marriage like our parents' marriages."

Peter broke in, "Both of us have always worked professionally, and for the first six years of our marriage we ate all our meals out."

"How did you feel about that?" I inquired.

"I loved it. I wrote a restaurant guide. I didn't want her to feel trapped by domesticity."

Susan added, "I had my own separate bank account for years. It was important for me to know I wasn't dependent."

In talking about his family and formative years, Peter told this story: "Once, when I was about eight, we lived for a short time with my paternal grandparents. Grandmother got the whole family together and said awful things about my mother. Mother pleaded with my dad to speak up for her, but he wouldn't. My sister and I were in the next room, crying. I vowed that nobody would ever do that to someone I loved! I now understand that this kind of behavior in my family is the energy behind my political passion for the underdog."

In response to my inquiry about her family background, Susan said she sees her mother as a very bright woman who did not have the opportunity for higher education. She feels that her mother denied being dissatisfied with the traditional female role, though her mother was expected by her husband to play that role and, in fact, *herself* expected to play it! Openly expressing dissatisfaction with her mother's model of womanhood, Susan noted that she herself, in many ways, had created the kind of marriage she thinks her mother really wanted — which includes full self-expression and a loving partner.

What about Peter's and Susan's own family? They have a grown son, and this is how Susan described raising him: "We set up our household to avoid bickering. We both hate bickering! We talked with him about his rules, and sometimes he changed our minds. We learned a lot from him. We raised him with the belief that Peter and I each live our own lives for ourselves rather than for him. He respects that. We never criticized him, but he developed his own inner critic, as we had. Now he is mature for his years — intuitive and balanced and a good student."

Susan pulled a birthday card from her purse. In careful printing, her son had composed a note full of appreciation for her, both as a person and as a mother.

Before I left them I asked one more question: "What do you think are the most important ingredients in your success as a couple?"

Peter answered first. "The most important thing is that we fill each other's deepest needs to be loved, valued, and appreciated. We never attack each other in any way."

Susan added, "We both want and need love. It's so precious to us that we wouldn't do anything to spoil it or dishonor it or jeopardize it. We like feeling in love so much that we nurture that feeling. Touching is important to us." They were holding hands at the table, looking very much in love.

Susan continued, "Our relationship is the foundation for our work and our success. Everything was harder before we met. It was hard trying to find a relationship and work at the same time."

Peter agreed. "I think talking things through at once and never allowing negativity to accumulate was important for us. Not that we don't have disagreements. But we made a rule early in our marriage that we wouldn't go to bed on a disagreement. And we spent some sleepless nights in the early years, because talking it out was important."

What can be learned from this inspiring pair? I am impressed with the fresh awareness they brought to their relationship. Rather than modeling their marriage on the traditional roles they saw around them, they carefully and thoughtfully constructed it so it met their own individual needs. Their childhoods had not been ideal, yet their families served as springboards for their relationship in important ways. Although their families had different religious backgrounds, the basic values and problems of those families were similar. Susan and Peter kept the positive values and used the problems to create something that worked better for them.

Both were determined to appreciate and nurture each other's individuality rather than to relive the emotional dependency of their parents. They forged many rules or boundaries through long discussions. They not only respected their own and each other's individuality, but they also created an individual relationship different from those of their original families and from the "norm" around them. Their obvious vitality and love continues to spread to the lives they touch.

The power of family and cultural patterns to provide a springboard for change and growth is expressed in this heretofore unpublished poem written by a friend of mine:

The Heritage

I speak not of you, my sweet mother.

*When I curse, I curse the centuries of oppression that weighed
you to the floor and held you there in its vise with me in your
arms and your mother before you and hers before her and hers
before.*

*I rail not against you, my father, but against the slavery in your
genes that destined you to enslave me as you were enslaved by
those before and ever since.*

*I turn away not to discredit your noble effort to show me how
to live your dream. I turn away to honor that dream by awak-
ening from it and standing upon your shoulders even as they
shake. I bless and praise your dreary struggle that fed this
passion in my soul to forge where you would never dare.*

*From this alien view, I can see you and those who have gone
before and your hearts are clapping and your eyes are dancing
in the joy of our flight. Because you know you are with me. And
you know that just for moments, we are free. At long last, just
for moments, we are free.*

—Sarah Edwards

Having studied your family patterns and gained some fresh insights,
how can you now put your new awareness into action in your life and
create your own wonderful relationship? Insights are valuable only if they
lead to behavioral changes. Here is a summary and review of important
suggestions:

1. *Heal yourself.* The hurts that painful experiences in your life have
inflicted upon you can be healed. Do not wait for a partner to "make it all
better." To feel good about yourself, do your own personal growing,
grieving, and learning. This may be done through reading, personal

writing, classes or workshops, or individual or group therapy. Objectivity about your relationships in your childhood family can help. Have discussions with old friends and family members.

2. *Observe the ways you may sabotage relationships.* Instead of blaming a partner, look at the way you unconsciously create the situations you fear. If you catch yourself thinking "all men are . . . " or "all women are . . . ," look deep inside yourself (perhaps with the assistance of another person) to see how your expectation causes you to behave in such a way as to create the very kind of relationship you fear. This kind of insight takes self-honesty and courage. It is not easy, which is why you may find that having help is useful.

3. *Stretch your limits in new situations.* If emotional intimacy is fearful for you, stay with a scary situation a little longer. Take small risks. If self-reliance is what you lack, take risks in doing things alone. If you look for beauty or success as criteria for a partner and thus have not found one, try looking for other qualities instead. Join new groups of people. Do some social things that are a little uncomfortable, a stretch in a growing direction.

4. *Choose to be with people who are emotionally healthy and growth-oriented.* Recognize the following trap, conscious or unconscious: "I will love him [her] so much that he [she] is bound to change." We can change as a result of a relationship, but not according to another's agenda. Would you want someone to plan for you to change according to his or her particular formula? Probably not. The stated mutual intention to support each other's wants, needs, and growth is healthy, quite different from the unstated intention to change each other.

5. *Identify your own major emotional trap or traps.* What is the one pattern or quality that has created the most pain in your relationships? For example, "My mother was critical. I could never be quite good enough. And I've chosen partners who helped me recapture that old familiar feeling." You may still be attracted to people who bring up that feeling, but the extent of the difficulty for you will lessen as you grow on your own. Learning and experiencing that an exciting, challenging relationship is possible with less of this familiar trap would provide a wonderful

release. To recognize the trap is to take the first step toward attracting something new and better. (The exercises in this book can help you with such a recognition.)

6. *Learn to recognize the components of friendship.* One of the most important features of a satisfying romantic relationship is that you are true friends. Friends enjoy each other, trust each other, share with each other, and have fun together. Of course, nonromantic friendships — whether same-sex or opposite-sex ones — also give you the opportunity to experience healthy relating and are very important.

A happy, healthy, robust relationship is something we all aspire to create. Though it does not happen by accident, *it is something you can have.* Thus, I want to conclude with a visualization about your future. You may want to have someone read this to you as you make yourself comfortable and imagine all of the elements of your life—yourself, your environment, and your relationships—exactly the way you want them to be.

EXERCISE 9: FUTURE VISUALIZATION

Close your eyes. Imagine yourself five years from now. Look at your face and hair . . . . How do you feel as a five-years-older person . . . ? Notice your body and your clothes . . . . How do you feel about yourself?

Now notice the outside of the place where you live. (You may choose the place you now live—perhaps with some alterations—or somewhere else.) Is it in the city or the country . . . ? At the mountains . . . the beach . . . ? Is it an apartment, a house, or something else . . . ? What is growing around it . . . ? Grass, potted plants, trees, flowers . . . ? What do you see from the front . . . ? Sky, skyscrapers, other homes, nature . . . ?

Now go inside. What colors do you see . . . ? What is the style or feeling of the decor . . . ? How is the home arranged to accommodate the priorities of your lifestyle . . . ? Is there adequate space for you or for you and your romantic partner . . . ? Are there spaces for work, for children, for pets, for other companions, for entertaining . . . ? How do these surroundings reflect your life at this time . . . ?

Now imagine the other or others who live in this place with you. Is a romantic partner living with you . . . ? What is he/she like . . . ? Energy level . . . ? Age . . . ? Appearance . . . ? Interests . . . ? Family . . . ? Traditions . . . ? Other values . . . ? How do you feel when you are with this friend/lover/partner . . . ?

Imagine a private meal with the people in your home. Who is there . . . ? Who has cooked the meal . . . ? Is there laughter, conversation, music . . . ? Or is it quiet . . . ? How do you feel in this atmosphere you have created . . . ? Imagine entertaining others in this home. Would this be a large group, a small group, or an intimate time for two . . . ?

Now imagine a day of work or useful activity. See yourself beginning your tasks. What excites you . . . ? Challenges you . . . ? How do you feel as you complete those tasks . . . ?

Imagine the end of your day has come. You are ready to relax and go to bed. Are you alone or with a partner . . . ? How do you feel . . . ? What is the quality of your relationship with yourself . . . ? With your partner . . . ? How does it feel to crawl into bed . . . ? And how does it feel to wake up in the morning in this home, with this person, or alone . . . ?

Now leave this time of your life and go forward to your eightieth birthday . . . . It is evening and you are celebrating in your home, in your own style . . . . Who is there with you . . . ? Family, friends, neighbors . . . ? What is most important to you . . . ?

Imagine that someone asks you the following questions: "Are you contented with the way you have lived your life?" "Have you loved and been loved the way you dreamed about when you were younger?" "If you could go back and do things over, what would you change . . . ?"

Complete the experience of your future. When you're ready, open your eyes. You may want to take a pencil and write down the things you can do now to ensure that you have the future of your dreams.

What one thing can you do this week to further your vision?

Go for it!

BIBLIOGRAPHY

Axline, Virginia M. *Play Therapy.* New York: Ballantine. 1969.

Bach, George R., and Ronald Deutsch. *Pairing.* New York: Avon Books. 1971.

Bach, George R., and Peter Wyden. *The Intimate Enemy: How to Fight Fair in Love and Marriage.* New York: Avon Books. 1970.

Bader, Ellyn, and Peter Pearson. *In Quest of the Mythical Mate: A Developmental Approach to Diagnosis and Treatment in Couples Therapy.* New York: Brunner/Mazel. 1988.

Balswick, Jack. *The Inexpressive Male.* Lexington: Lexington Books. 1988.

Barbach, Lonnie, and David L. Geisinger. *Going the Distance: Finding and Keeping Lifelong Love.* New York: Plume. 1993.

Bernard, Jesse. *The Future of Marriage.* New York: Bantam Books, 1973.

Brinkley, Ginny, Linda Goldberg, and Janice Kukar. *Your Child's First Journey: A Guide to Prepared Birth from Pregnancy to Parenthood.* Wayne: Avery. 1982.

Boszormenyi-Nagy, Ivan, and Geraldine M. Spark. *Invisible Loyalties.* New York: Harper and Row. 1973.

Bradshaw, John E. *Bradshaw on Family.* Deerfield Beach: Health Communications. 1987.

Brazelton, T. Berry. *Infants and Mothers.* New York: Del Publishing Co. 1983.

Brown, Molly Young. *The Unfolding Self: Psychosynthesis and Counseling.* Los Angeles: Psychosynthesis Press. 1983.

Campbell, Susan M. *Beyond the Power Struggle.* San Luis Obispo: Impact. 1984.

―――. *The Couple's Journey: Intimacy as a Path to Wholeness.* San Luis Obispo: Impact. 1980.

Carter, E., and M. McGoldrick. *The Family Life Cycle: A Framework for Family Therapy.* New York: Gardner Press. 1980.

Castine, Jacqueline. *Recovery from Rescuing.* Deerfield Beach: Health Communications, Inc. 1989.

Cowan, Connell, and Melvyn Kinder. *Women Men Love, Women Men Leave.* New York: Signet. 1988.

Coyle-Hennessey, Bobbi. *Once More with Love: A Guide to Marrying Again.* Notre Dame: Ave Maria Press. 1993.

Curran, Dolores. *Traits of a Healthy Family.* Minneapolis: Winston. 1983.

Davidson, Joy. *The Agony of It All: The Drive for Drama and Excitement in Women's Lives.* Los Angeles: Tarcher. 1988.

DeAngelis, Barbara. *Are You the One for Me?* New York: Delacorte. 1992.

Diamond, Jed. *Looking for Love in All the Wrong Places: Overcoming Romantic and Sexual Addictions.* New York: Putnam's. 1988.

Dinkmeyer, Don, and Gary D. McKay. *The Parent's Handbook.* 3rd ed. Circle Pines: American Guidance Service.

Dowling, Collette. *The Cinderella Complex.* New York: Pocket. 1982.

Estes, Clarissa Pinkola. *Women Who Run with the Wolves.* New York: Ballentine. 1992.

Faludi, Susan. *Backlash: The Undeclared War against American Women.* New York: Anchor. 1991.

Farrell, Warren. *Why Men Are the Way They Are.* New York: McGraw-Hill. 1986.

Felder, Leonard A. *A Fresh Start: How to Let Go of Emotional Baggage and Enjoy Your Life Again.* New York: NAL Penguin. 1987.

Firestone, Robert W. *The Fantasy Bond.* New York: Human Sciences Press. 1987.

Fisher, Bruce. *Rebuilding: When Your Relationship Ends.* San Luis Obispo: Impact. 1987.

Fisher, Robert. *The Knight in Rusty Armor.* North Hollywood: Wilshire Book Co. 1990.

Forward, Susan. *Men Who Hate Women and the Women Who Love Them.* New York: Bantam. 1987.

Framo, James L. *Explorations in Marital and Family Therapy.* New York: Springer. 1982.

Gray, John. *Men Are fom Mars, Women Are fom Venus.* New York: HarperCollins. 1992.

————. *What Your Mother Couldn't Tell You and Your Father Didn't Know.* New York: HarperCollins. 1994.

Haley, Jay. *Problem-Solving Therapy: New Strategies for Effective Family Therapy.* New York: HarperColophon. 1978.

Halpern, Howard. *How to Break Your Addiction to a Person.* New York: Bantam. 1983.

Harding, Christopher, ed. *Wingspan: Inside the Men's Movement.* New York: St. Martin's. 1992.

Hendrix, Harville. *Getting the Love You Want: A Guide for Couples.* New York: Holt. 1988.

Hotchner, Tracy. *Pregnancy and Childbirth.* New York: Holt. 1984.

James, John, and Ibis Schlesinger. *Are You the One for Me?* Reading: Addison-Wesley. 1987.

James, Muriel, and Dorothy Jongeward. *Born to Win: Transactional Analysis with Gestalt Experiments.* Reading: Addison-Wesley. 1971.

Jampolsky, Gerald G. *Love Is Letting Go of Fear.* Millbrae: Celestial Arts. 1979.

Jeffers, Susan. *Opening Our Hearts to Men.* New York: Fawcett Columbine. 1989.

Keen, Sam. *Fire in the Belly: On Being a Man.* New York: Bantam. 1991.

King, Vivian. *Inner Theatre Playbook: An Interactive Guide to Personal Change.* Santa Fe: Spirit Mountain Productions. 1994.

Kipnis, Aaron, and Elizabeth Herron. *Gender War, Gender Peace: The Quest for Love and Justice Between Women and Men.* New York: Morrow. 1994.

————. *Knights without Armor: A Practical Guide for Men in Quest of Masculine Soul.* Los Angeles: Tarcher. 1991.

Kritzberg, Wayne. *The Adult Children of Alcoholics Syndrome.* Pompano Beach: Health Communications. 1985.

Kübler-Ross, Elisabeth. *On Death and Dying.* New York: Macmillan. 1976.

Kuriansky, Judy. *How to Love a Nice Guy.* New York: Doubleday. 1990.

Lederman, Ellen. *Perfect Partners: The Couples' Compatibility Guide.* New York: Pocket. 1990.

Lemen, Kevin. *The Birth Order Book: Why You Are the Way You Are.* New York: Dell. 1984.

————. *Living in a Step Family without Getting Stepped On.* Nashville, Atlanta: Thomas Nelson Publishers. 1994.

Mayer, Nancy. *The Male Mid-life Crisis.* New York: New American Library. 1979.

Miller, Alice. *The Drama of the Gifted Child.* New York: Basic Books. 1981.

Minuchin, Salvador. *Families and Family Therapy.* Cambridge: Harvard. 1980.

Montagu, Ashley. *Touching: The Human Significance of the Skin.* New York: Harper and Row. 1986.

Moore, Robert, and Douglas Gillette. *King, Warrior, Magician, Lover: Rediscovering the Archetypes of the Mature Masculine.* San Francisco: Harper. 1990.

Moseley, Douglas, and Naomi Moseley. *Dancing in the Dark: The Shadow Side of Intimate Relationships.* Georgetown: North Star. 1994.

Moustakas, C. E. *Psychotherapy with Children: The Living Relationship.* New York: Harper and Row. 1979.

Napier, Augustus Y. *The Fragile Bond: In Search of an Equal, Intimate and Enduring Marriage.* New York: Harper and Row. 1988.

Papernow, Patricia. *Becoming a Stepfamily: Patterns of Development in Remarried Families.* San Francisco: Jossey-Bass. 1993.

Paul, Jordan, and Margaret Paul. *Do I Have to Give Up Me to Be Loved by You?* Minneapolis: CompCare. 1983.

——. *Free to Love.* Los Angeles: Evolving Publications. 1983.

Paul, Norman, and Betty Byfield Paul. *A Marital Puzzle.* New York: Gardner. 1986.

Peck, M. Scott. *The Road Less Traveled.* New York: Simon and Schuster. 1979.

Perls, Frederick S. *In and Out of the Garbage Pail.* Lafayette: Real People Press. 1969.

Probstein, Bobbie. *Return to Center.* Marina Del Rey: DeVorss. 1985.

Satir, Virginia, and Michelle Baldwin. *Satir Step by Step.* Palo Alto: Science and Behavior Books. 1983.

——. *The Use of Self in Therapy.* New York: Hayworth. 1987.

Satir, Virginia. *Conjoint Family Therapy.* Palo Alto: Science and Behavior Books. 1983.

——. *Peoplemaking.* Palo Alto: Science and Behavior Books. 1972.

Scarf, Maggie. *Intimate Partners.* New York: Ballantine. 1988.

Schnarch, David M. *Constructing the Sexual Crucible: An Integration of Sexual and Marital Therapy.* New York: Norton. 1991.

Sills, Judith. *How to Stop Looking for Someone Perfect and Find Someone to Love.* New York: Ballantine. 1984.

Slater, Philip. *The Pursuit of Loneliness.* Boston: Beacon. 1971.

Stone, Hal, and Sidra Stone. *Embracing Each Other: Relationship as Teacher, Healer and Guide.* San Rafael: New World Library. 1989.

——. *Embracing Our Selves: The Voice Dialogue Manual.* San Rafael: New World Library. 1989.

——. *Embracing Your Inner Critic: Turning Self-Criticism into a Creative Asset.* San Francisco: Harper. 1993.

Thomas, Alexander, and Stella Chess. *Temperament and Behavior Disorders in Children.* New York: Basic Books. 1968.

Viorst, Judith. *Necessary Losses: The Love Illusions, Dependencies and Impossible Expectations That All of Us Have to Give Up in Order to Grow.* New York: Fawcett. 1987.

Wallerstein, Judith, and Sandra Blakeslee. *The Good Marriage: How and Why Love Lasts.* Boston, New York: Houghton Mifflin. 1995.

————. *Second Chances: Men, Women and Children a Decade after Divorce.* New York: Tichnor Fields. 1989.

Whitfield, Charles. *Healing the Child Within.* Pompano Beach: Health Communications. 1987.

INDEX

DANCING IN THE DARK
The Shadow Side of Intimate Relationships
Douglas & Naomi Moseley

"Bravo! Brava! Finally a book with real solutions for real relationships . . . a must-read for individuals, couples, and helping professionals."
— Pat Love, Ed.D.; co-author, Hot Monogamy

" . . . an invaluable resource for understanding the full range of life's most rigorous spiritual practice: the art and craft of relationship."
— Angeles Arrien, Ph.D.; author, The Four-Fold Way, Signs of Life

"Dancing in the Dark is rare. The difficult and emotionally charged aspects of the shadow side of relationships are covered with clarity and thoroughness. I can easily recommend [it] to the professional and lay readership."
— Harold D. Holder, Ph.D.
Director and Senior Scientist, Prevention Research Center

RIDING THE DRAGON
The Power of Committed Relationship
Rhea Powers & Gawain Bantle

"A radically fresh, challenging and inspired path into vastly expanded personal and mutual development attainable through a committed relationship."
— W. Brugh Joy, M.D.; author, Joy's Way, Avalanche

"A wise, bold, honest map through the maze of intimate relationship. Rhea and Gawain are delightful mirrors, reflecting hope, courage and inspiration for all lovers."
— Gabrielle Roth, author Maps to Ecstasy: Teachings of an Urban Shaman

"An exceptional and insightful book that offers ground breaking insights on the most difficult of life's challenges — fostering deep and meaningful relationships."
— Beth S. Jarman, Ph.D.; author, Breakpoint and Beyond